Doctor
Always On Call

Doctor
Always On Call

The Life Of Robert H. Morris, M.D.
As Told To His Son, Rober H. Morris II

Robert H. Morris

ARPress
ILLUMINATING IDEAS.
EMPOWERING VOICES

ARPress
45 Dan Road Suite 5
Canton MA 02021

Hotline: 1(888) 821-0229
Fax: 1(508) 545-7580

Ordering Information:

Quantity sales. Special discounts are available on quantity purchases by corporations, associations, and others. For details, contact the publisher at the address above.

Printed in the United States of America.

ISBN-13:   Softcover   979-8-89330-128-1
            eBook   979-8-89330-130-4
            Hardcover   979-8-89330-129-8

Library of Congress Control Number: 2024901207

Information about External Hyperlinks in this ebook

Please note that footnotes in this ebook may contain hyperlinks to external websites as part of bibliographic citations. These hyperlinks have not been activated by the publisher, who cannot verify the accuracy of these links beyond the date of publication.

Frontispiece: Robert H. Morris, M.D., at age 39. On back is written: "Robert Morris 2/9/44 To My Dad." At this point, Dr. Morris had been in Medina almost seven years and had four children; his fifth and last child would be born just nine months later. Made at Farley's Portrait Studio in Chattanooga, Tennessee, apparently on a visit to Dr. Steven Byars' family.

The publishers of Dr. Robert Morris's autobiography dedicate it to his descendants now living and to those yet to be born, to his other relatives, to his medical colleagues, and to the people in and around Medina, Tennessee, whom he served and whose love sustained him.

**WHETHER LIFE GRINDS A MAN DOWN
OR POLISHES HIM UP
DEPENDS UPON THE STUFF
HE IS MADE OF**

(Printed on a card posted over Dr. Morris's desk for 25 years or more. The card is from "Moore Companies / Allied Laboratories, Inc."; the cancellation stamp reads "Jackson, Tennessee, July 4, 1945," and the address reads "Dr. R.H. Morris, M.D. / Medina, Tenn."

TABLE OF CONTENTS

PREFACE
To The Elm Hill Edition

Originally published in 1991 by our family as *Memories of a Small-Town Doctor*, a new title is needed because the first does not adequately convey the scope or depth of Dr. Robert Morris's medical practice. True, his life was centered in the small town or village xof Medina, Tennessee (pop. 400- 600 in the 1940s through the 1970s), but he made home visits from the 1930s up to about 1970 in five counties—the last doctor to do so in our area. During his career he delivered some 2500 babies, most of these in the home, and to this day I meet people who fondly recall that Dr. Morris delivered them. He was also on the staff of three small nearby hospitals (one of which he was a founding partner until he sold his shares, feeling he was over-extending himself) as well as of the regional Jackson General Hospital. His picture and a bronze plaque with his name hung in the Jackson General "Hall of Fame" until the "hall" itself was removed some years ago during renovation. One year he was president of the consolidated medical association.

When he sent patients to these hospitals, he followed up by visiting them there; they were still *his* patients. The shingle outside his office billed his services as "Medicine and Minor Surgery," but in the hospitals he helped in the ER, administered anesthesia, and assisted surgeons in major operations.

During World War II, he served the military by examining men as to their fitness for service, and did the same for personnel hired at the Milan Arsenal, a major ammunition plant just five miles away.

Dad charged low fees: $1 for a prescription, $3 for a full physical exam, $3 to $7 for a home visit, which might be 20 miles or more away. Payment sometimes was in the form of a watermelon or a cured ham. He charged $25 for a home delivery, involving multiple visits, and during the actual delivery he served as nurse as well, sitting hours by the patient's side. I think that he identified with the poor farmers, black and white, who constituted the majority of his patients. In fact, he carried debts on his books for many years, and did not pursue the patients for payment unless he saw that they bought a new car or had increased their income without paying him. My four sisters and I picked cotton in the fall and bought most of our own school clothes. We thought Dad was downright stingy; we had to beg and wheedle to get a dime or quarter out of him for anything. He tithed his income, spent sparingly, invested in whole life insurance policies and in stocks—for the most part wisely—and in the end left Lillie, his wife, a nice nest-egg which, after her death, came largely intact to us children. But he didn't aim at being rich. In his will he declared, "All debts are forgiven." These, in the year of his death, 1990, may have amounted to some $100,000.

A devout Christian and Southern Baptist, Dad attended all services, chaired the deacon board, taught a men's Bible class for over 50 years, and at times sang in the choir. I often walked to his office, three blocks from our house, and if no patients were there, he would either be reading medical journals or preparing to teach his Sunday School lesson. He supported Bible teaching ministries he felt were sound, such as J. Vernon McGee and Billy Graham. He wasn't saintly, but if he had a problem with someone, he would confront him face to face, try to resolve the issue, then drop it.

Dad was not a workaholic. A regular nap after lunch helped keep his body in balance. Although toughened to hard work on the farm as a boy, he loved to relax. As a young man he played the piano. He played basketball in his youth, and baseball past the age of 40, until he broke his heel bone. Rarely he might go hunting or fishing with friends. He played bridge with professional colleagues and neighbors. In later years, he enjoyed watching sports on TV, and he went to some football bowl games with friends. He loved to sit and tell stories, stories full of pain and humor, which gave me the idea for this book. He last worked a crop on the farm at age 26, and after settling in Medina grew a large and beautifully-kept garden that provided produce for his family of seven; he found this relaxing. In his 50s he once borrowed a mule, plow, and harrow, and broke up and harrowed his garden, proving he hadn't forgotten his farming skills. One time Dad made a trip to Washington, D.C., with his father, and in later years two trips out west with his wife and friends. The farthest he got was to Tijuana, Mexico, the only time he stepped foot outside the U.S. I recall him saying that once there he felt convicted that his patients needed him, so he took the next train back home, cutting the trip short.

In 1950 he built a neat, modest brick office, designed by Lillie, his artistic wife (a registered nurse), where he kept regular hours, with Saturday afternoons and Sundays off—but even those times subject to interruption by patients in need. I can personally verify that many times phone calls came in the middle of the night: "Doc, my wife's going into labor" or, "Doc, something's wrong with my baby. He's having trouble breathing." Dad might protest at first that it could wait till morning, but if the patient persisted, he'd always get up and go. And when he returned, he'd go back to bed, then rise at his regular time, splash cold water on his face three times, shave, read the Bible and the newspaper while smoking (a habit he picked up at age 12 and only laid down in his 70s), eat breakfast, and start a new day. He was always on call. He had no backup or replacement. The health of the community was primarily on his shoulders alone.

Robert H. Morris II

FOREWORD
by Robert Morris II, and Letters from Each of His Children

This book originated in the desire to give something back to my father at the end of his life, and in the conviction that his memories not only make an interesting story, but are worth preserving for the future.

In July 1988, I enjoyed several days with my parents in Medina, Tennessee, and spent a good portion of that time recording some six hours of interviews with Dad (then in his 84th year) on audio cassettes. While wanting memories of Dad's life, I wasn't sure exactly what I would do with them.

Over the next 14 months, as I transcribed these recordings, the core of a book emerged. I attempted to shape it into a connected, first-person narrative. Mother and my four sisters supported me both morally and financially; they joined me, when we gathered to celebrate his 85th birthday in September, 1989, in presenting to Dad the first draft of what would become, if he chose to work with me, his autobiography. I read my letter of dedication to him, as did each of his daughters. (These letters conclude our foreword, except that, following Dad's death, Trebor has exercised the option of replacing her original letter with a new one. For this reason I have placed it last.)

As I recall, Dad responded first by suggesting that there was no need for a book on his life; perhaps, too, he dreaded the task that lay before us, remembering how I had interfered with several days of TV viewing the year before. Nevertheless, he worked with me over the next three days, as much as family and birthday well-wishers allowed. Our final recordings were made in the car as we drove together to the Nashville airport, where I was to board a plane for my return flight to Texas.

Over the following 14 months, Dad and I mailed chapters back and forth: I sent him the new and revised chapters as they were completed, and Mother helped him to read and correct them for me. This process continued until his final illness. In November 1990, less than a week before he was hospitalized and diagnosed as having cancer of the pancreas, I received a letter from him, in answer to my request, recounting the special service held at the First Baptist Church in Medina the previous April in which he had been honored. Then, when I visited him in the hospital perhaps two weeks after this, he gave me minimal responses to a couple of questions relative to the book, and that was his last participation in it.

Following Dad's death on December 27, 1990, I have felt a new urgency to bring this work to completion. Copy originally typed into a word processor has been fed into my new computer to help in final editing. Our earlier approach of a shoestring operation has been discarded in favor of professional typesetting and quality binding, using funds Mother has made available from the estate.

Although Dad narrated and reviewed most of the material in this book, I bear the responsibility, as the final editor, for faithfully recording the truth about him. I have tried to make his language clearer and easier to read without burying his personality and style of expression. I have resisted— hopefully with some success—any temptation to remake Dad in my own image or to cater to the sentiments of others. I hope the result is faithful to Dad's character and to the reality of who he was. I hope it will serve not only our family but the community as well, for his life is part of its history.

I loved Dad, and I always knew he loved me. Even when our disagreements were marked by anger and tears, love bound us together. To me Dad was neither a "saint" (as that term is commonly used of an especially pious or self-sacrificing person), nor a "giant" in sensational courage or heroic deeds. His faults were not hard to find—he could be irritable, dogmatic, pessimistic, and demanding. Still, a fair appraisal will credit him with having "substance," as a man and as a Christian. He was an honest person—paying debts, keeping his word, telling the truth. He had integrity—faithful to his church and to his understanding of God, loyal to his family and friends. He knew how to forgive and overlook past offenses.

He was generous financially, certainly to his family, his church, his alma mater, and to ministries he considered to be valid. I am impressed with his commitment to relationships: He maintained a vigorous correspondence with distant friends and spent much time with both family and friends in the community.

Dad was accustomed from childhood to hard work. Until his retirement he had few real vacations other than Sundays off, and even they were often interrupted by requests for his services. Dad was devoted to the art of medicine and to his calling as a physician; until the end he maintained an active interest in medical advances and changes. While his was a family practice in general medicine and surgery, he had the respect of his specialist colleagues, especially as a diagnostician. His last prescription was written just weeks before his death.

I have overruled a request from a few individuals to alter the title to *Memories of a GREAT Small-Town Doctor*. Since, in spite of our "doctoring," this remains Dad's *autobiography*, I reason that we cannot use a title he would not have accepted; and he was modest. In addition, I have a problem with the word "great": Besides its vagueness, it suggests someone either widely famous or otherwise "larger than life"; and Dad was neither. But I agree that he deserves honor, and with the feeling that, in some ways, he *was* an outstanding doctor and an extraordinary man. Excerpts from an obituary by Erica Berry[1] will illustrate his qualities as a physician and as a person:

> [Finis] Sims recalled Morris referred him to surgeons several years ago for a series of operations Morris couldn't handle himself, but Morris still went to the hospital with him four times....
>
> "He could diagnose a case before you could turn around," said [Stacy] Davenport. "He had one of the sharpest brains I've ever seen."...
>
> Morris was a "patient's doctor," said Dr. G. Baker Hubbard, a Jackson physician who retired in January. Morris always kept up with changes in modern medicine and genuinely cared about his patients.... "He showed

an interest in his patients and they loved him," said Hubbard....

"His colleagues said he always had the right diagnosis and they just confirmed it," Mrs. [Lillie] Morris said.

In his early days as a physician, Morris made many house calls and believed in going that extra mile to help those who needed it.... "He thought enough of you to come by before you even called, if he knew you were sick," Davenport said.

Besides his medical skills, Davenport recalls Morris as a "good Christian man."

"Morally he was one of the most honest people you'd ever know," she said.

I will let the record speak for itself, and let you, the reader, reach your own conclusions about Robert Morris, M.D.

A number of family members and friends have been genuinely helpful in this project, and I want to thank them here: Mother participated from the sidelines when I made the first recordings, and has functioned as an assistant editor ever since, correcting and supplementing Dad's memories and contributing to overall design. All of my sisters—Una Grant, Trebor Ambrose, Brenda Nulter, and Lillie Cate—and their spouses have supported my efforts morally and financially. Also, each sister has scanned the text for errors, especially helping to correct and update the chapters on "Home Life" and on "Our Children, Grandchildren, and Great-Grandchildren." Cherie (Grant) Morgan and Christy Cate, granddaughters of Dr. Morris, also served as proofreaders. Dad's sister, Evelyn Key; his brothers, John and Guy Morris; and Jean Mausehund, his nephew Bobby Joe Mincey's widow (now remarried), helped correct and update the chapter on "My Sister and Brothers." John Morris, at my request, reviewed all the chapters up to Dad entering medical school, and Sue (Morgan) Morris, Guy's wife, helped straighten me out on the history of Gibson Baptist Church. Terry Blount kindly made several copies of the manuscript for the family; further, he and his wife, Marsha, proofread the entire manuscript and corrected several typos and misspelled names. Joel

Bradbury and Edwin Todd of Medina caught many errors in the spelling of names, for which I am grateful. Thanks to the *Medina Star* for permission to reprint and adapt several articles; to the *Jackson Sun* for permission to excerpt Dad's obituary; to the Lee-Davis U.D.C. Historical Society for permission to adapt a paragraph from their *Families and History of Gibson County, Tennessee, to 1989.* Thanks to my employer, G&S Typesetters, Inc., of Austin, Texas, for typesetting this book on favorable terms, and to those of my colleagues who took a personal interest in its production. Finally, thanks to my wife, Jeanne, and to our children for accepting the sacrifices that this project has required of them.

A note to the reader: Throughout this book I generally have abbreviated my own name, Robert Hunt Morris II, as "RMII"; likewise I have abbreviated Mother's name, Lillie May (Leake) Morris, as "LLM."

I close with my own letter to Dad, slightly edited here from hand-written notes, which I read to him on September 23, 1989, as we presented the first draft of this book to him:

> *Dear Dad,*
>
> *We've gathered today to celebrate your 85 years of life and to thank you for imparting life to us.*
>
> *What we've chosen to do collectively to mark this occasion is to begin the process of putting the story of your life, and your memories, into print, so that the heritage you received from your parents and grandparents, which we know to be so precious to you, as well as your own experiences, will be preserved for us and for generations to come.*
>
> *Your memories reach back to include Dr. Hunt's recollections of the Civil War and its aftermath. They include your own youth, spent in a world that is radically different from ours today: your whole existence confined to the local community of Gibson, with occasional trips to Humboldt [seven miles away]; even Jackson [about 20 miles away] seemed a big town far away; and going to Memphis [100 miles away] was like going to another country. Dirt roads; only horses, buggies, and wagons for transportation; no cars, no radios, no electricity.*

*In that world, which today seems so far away and long ago, you knew of hard work, simple pleasures, and strict morality. You **were** torn between the desire to stay in the safety of this small world and the desire to develop and use the talents God gave you, and to move into a larger and more complex world. There are a lot of stories to tell along the way, most of them funny in retrospect, but many of them actually involving a lot of pain.*

As I have worked on transcribing and editing the six hours of your memories that we recorded in July 1988, I have agonized with you as twice you dropped out of medical school; have tasted your victory in going back to lead your class in seven out of 12 semesters, in obtaining the coveted internship at Memphis General Hospital, in wooing and wedding your sweet woman who has faithfully stood with you these 50 years and more; and have recalled my own life emerging from the Medina community in the context of World War II, the Milan Arsenal, your seven-days-a-week medical practice, and the religious devotion and division in our home.

*... We present to you today this first typescript of what will become, with your participation, your autobiography.... We might entitle it **Memories of a Small-Town Doctor**....*

*I'm hoping that during my few days with you now, you will work with me on correcting as much of this first draft as possible. Whatever we cannot cover before I leave, I hope you will go **over** with Mother and mail to me later. When new material is introduced that involves more than a few lines, I'll record your words now and edit them at [my own] home. As I process the corrections, I will mail you sections of the book for final proofreading and ask you to mail them back to me with further corrections....*

When we had reached the airport in Nashville that day in September 1989, knowing I had recorded practically all the material I needed for his autobiography and also aware that I might not see Dad again, or at most a few more times before his death, I burst into tears and said something like this: "Dad, I want you to know that when you are gone we won't forget you, and that what you have believed in won't be lost." The core of Dad's being, the truth around which his life revolved, was his faith in Jesus as Savior and Lord. This faith continued to polish him up until the end, even as age and illness ground his body down. I'm thankful that such a man was my father.

Robert Hunt Morris II

Dear Dad,

One of my very early positive memories is the day our **Harvard Classics** *arrived. It was a happy time. I could not have been more than three years (and likely less). I stood in a chair by the eating- table; I think it may have been round. Anyhow, the big box* **was** *opened, and you took out the beautiful blue volumes one by one. (Mom* **was** *there too.) I was instructed in the art of breaking in new books. This seemed to take so-o-o long, and I was anxious to get on with seeing all of them. Today I appreciate good literature, but have found no writings which can surpass the inspired scriptures.*

Your approach to life has been, seemingly to me, from the depth of pain. I long tried to struggle with that, and got so caught up in your pain that it took many years before I got in touch with my own and **was** *able to start thoroughly working on myself. God is good. He lets us help each other, especially those we love. We always knew your feelings were for us and our eternal life with Christ Jesus. Had my experiences been different, my breakthrough to God and my joy would not have been so complete.*

Thanks for making it possible for me to stay in Memphis, the town where Craig, myself, and our children **all grew** *up. This town has provided very positive opportunities for our unique talents and goals. Gibson, Medina, and Memphis— culture, love, and training!*

Thanks for it all,
Una D.

[written] July 22, 1989

Dad,

Some are born with such positive, cheerful spirits, and some of us must continually "fight" the helm to keep our ship aright. Perhaps the longer I live the more I understand others, especially my father. I continually remind myself that one-half my genes are from him, and half my children's genes are from me. This reminder keeps me with a more understanding spirit towards myself and my fellowman... No matter what cards we've been dealt, it is how we play the game—win or lose.

Dad, you are one of the people I admire the most because you played the game so well:

1. Few can set goals and deny themselves in order to reach them as well as you;
2. Your love for structure and order keep you to a routine that makes you very productive and successful;
3. You are very generous to your children in need but do not demand what is rightfully yours;
4. You love right, and honesty and truthfulness are always your policy.

I would indeed be honored if my children could bestow on me these same compliments.

With love,
Your "middle child"
Brenda

Sept. 26, 1989

Dear Mom and Dad,

I have learned from you a love for God and a love for others. Because of your religious differences, I made a commitment at an early age to choose a mate of "like precious faith." I thank God daily for answering this prayer.

Mom and Dad, your differences have been easier to accept, knowing Mom changed several years after your marriage. This change was a result of her continual study and a conviction of God's Word, and not out of a disrespect to her mate.

Dad, you are a very honest person and admire this quality in others. You would not have had the strong respect you have for Mother if she had been dishonest to this conviction just to please you. Dad, you have seen Mother possess a "peace that passes understanding" due to her faith. This has allowed her to love you, respect you, and give you encouragement at times others would have given up due to your disposition.

Because of your commitment to God and one another, you have set an example that will encourage generations to come. We love you, and a "Happy 85th Birthday", Dad!

Lillie Cate
Your 5th Child

Charles, Tom, and Christy also join in this special birthday greeting.

[written] 2/10/91

Dr. Morris—My Dad

Three words which in my mind summarize my Dad would be God, medicine, and family. He was deeply committed to all three and instilled within me a great love and respect for the same.

His life was one which contained little self-indulgence. He was truly a servant—of God and man.

On the human side, he was by nature often irritable, and seldom felt comfortable enjoying luxuries or giving them to others—even to his own family. He was an avid student of both Bible and medicine throughout life.

Dad believed deeply in discipline and respect for authority. Providing for the education of his children was one of his primary physical goals. He filled our home with good literature and books of educational value. He also set an example of continual stimulation of the mind through reading and listening to others worthy of respect.

Dad's responsibilities as the spiritual leader of his home weighed heavily upon his heart. It was of grave concern to him that Mother's continued search for Truth, and faithfulness to her convictions, resulted in our home being divided religiously. He prayed faithfully and unashamedly for each of his children throughout life.

Dad approached most of life's situations through a negative point of view, which deprived him of much joy that should rightfully have been his. I told Mother at his death that I tended to be almost as positive a personality as Dad was a negative one, but we seemed to meet each other in the middle, sharing many of the same values and deep commitments. Dad seemed to enjoy the fact that my name was the same as his, spelled backwards. Our personality difference seems to suggest another way I was his "mirror image."

Needlework has often been for me a creative pastime and means of self-expression. The piece I chose to give Dad was as follows:

Dad

The seeds of love and wisdom
That you planted on my way
Have given me the roots to grow
And strengthened me each day.

Thank you, Dad!
Trebor

PART I

JOURNEY THROUGH LIFE

CHAPTER I

FAMILY BACKGROUND

I was born in the little town of Gibson, in Gibson County, Tennessee, on September 26, 1904, my parents being Joseph Edward Morris and Bernice Hunt Morris. My father's parents were John Peter Morris and Sarah Chandler Morris; my mother's parents were Dr. Robert Hardy Hunt and Lisa Hurt Hunt.[1] I do not know when my ancestors first settled in Gibson County, but understand that they originally came from North Carolina to the vicinity of what today is Eldad, Tennessee. I believe Dr. Hunt's parents had nine children: my great-uncles John, Wash, Matt, Joe, Elbert, and Willis, Hardy, and my great-aunts Fanny and Emma.

Most of my relatives were farmers. Elbert and Joe Hunt went out to Texas and homesteaded in what became Hunt County, and I never did see Uncle Elbert again. Uncle Joe came back one time on a visit, but I never saw any of his family. I heard that Elbert had 13 sons and that he died from sepsis (a putrefying infection) after skinning his heel on a plow. I think Uncle Joe had two sons—one who became a rancher and one who became a banker—and that they both lived in or around Palestine, Texas. Dr. Hunt's other brothers all stayed in West Tennessee.

Dr. Hunt

When the Civil War came, Joe and Matt, and maybe John and Wash too, joined the Confederate army. But my grandfather, Robert Hardy Hunt, was only 16 and still at home when the Yankees came to their farm, taking their feed and their best horses, leaving only their sorriest animals behind. The soldiers talked rough to his mother and father, provoking Robert Hardy so much that he told his parents he was going to kill them. But his parents said, "Oh, no! If you do that, they'll kill *us!*" So he said, "Well, I'll just join the army."

He enlisted with Forrest's Cavalry, whose mission at that point in time was to intercept Federal troops coming out of Memphis and stop them from meeting up with Grant. They did catch up with the Yankees in Mississippi, and fought them out from Tupelo in what has been called the Battle of Harrisburg.

Dr. Morris *(left)*, narrator of this book, and his brother John, standing, with Robert Morris II, writer and editor of this book, seated. They were visiting White Rose Cemetery in Gibson, Tennessee, the day after the family had surprised Dr. Morris with the first draft, and were obtaining dates of ancestors from tombstones. Photo by LLM.

I asked him one time: "Grandpa, could you see any of 'em?" "Oh, yeah, when the smoke would rise, you'd see 'em walking along." "Would you shoot?" "Yeah, just crack down on 'em!" "You reckon you killed any?" "I just don't know"; but he said the corn in that field was cut down just like it had been mowed. I also heard him say once that seven or eight boys from Gibson County were lying dead there on the ground after the battle. Forrest's Cavalry had the practice of letting one man out of every so many dismount and hold horses while the others fought. As I remember Grandpa telling it, the day that the battle occurred happened to be his day to handle the horses, but he traded places with someone, because sometimes the horses would stampede, and he would rather take his chances fighting. Grandpa had fired 30 rounds or so when he reached over in his pocket to get a mini-ball to reload, and a bullet struck him in the left elbow.

Furd Hudson found him on the battlefield and carried him on his horse to a big lawn. There he was bandaged up, and since he had lost so much blood, he was put in a boxcar and taken to Okolona, Mississippi.

At Okolona, Grandpa was carried to the operating table three times. The first time, they said, "Well, he's lost so much blood, he'll die anyway," so they didn't operate. The second time, he had an infection with gangrene, and they decided to burn it out with acid rather than operate. The third time, they said he couldn't stand an operation; he'd die anyway. But he said, "No, I'm going back home to Tennessee"— and he did. He went down and stayed with the Gays in Mississippi, and later (I don't know how many months later) he came home on a horse.

(As a teenager, I once rode with Grandpa to Shiloh National Military Park for Decoration Day. After spending the night in a nearby town, we got up early and toured the grounds. When Grandpa saw that the bodies of Confederate soldiers lay in unmarked trenches, while each Federal soldier had a marker, and some of the officers had tall marble monuments, he had me go back to the car with him and head straight home. I had to miss the bands and the decorated floats that were going to come down the Tennessee River later that day.)[2]

Back in Gibson County, Grandpa and his family had a hard life. Only their poorest animals, and strays that the Yankees didn't want, were left behind. They had to take these animals and try to make a crop, grazing them in the pastures and cane bottoms. They boiled the dirt under the smokehouse to get salt; they also parched corn and used that for coffee. Grandpa told me many a time: "Boy, you don't know what hard times are!"

Robert Hardy Hunt, M.D., maternal grandfather of Dr. Morris. R. H. Hunt was born in 1845 and fought in the Battle of Harrisburg at age 16. Someone has written "1873" on the reverse, but that would make the man in the picture only 28 years old, whereas he appears to be 48 or even older here.

The Hunt family worried about Robert Hardy. How was he going to make a living, since his arm wasn't healing and constantly bothered him? (In fact it never did fully heal; the skin would peel off and blood would ooze out. I think the shattered pieces of bone had worked out, and he actually broke his arm a second time in mid-life when Papa and some other men were trying to top some trees in front of his house. They had a rope attached to a limb; it was taut and Grandpa's arm was resting on it. The tree limb fell, jerking the rope up and popping his bone in two. But they put his arm in a right-angle splint, and it healed.)

Anyway, Grandpa finally went to medical school up in Nashville, received further training under a Doctor Turley (or some name like that),[3] then began practicing medicine on his own in Gibson. This he did for over 50 years.

When Grandpa first established himself as a doctor in Gibson, he lived in the third house down from where the school stands today. It is a frame building, probably one of the oldest houses in Gibson. Then he bought a farm of some 100 to 110 acres, across the street from where the school was later built, and in 1889 he constructed the white house that still stands today, later adding the columns and the wrap-around porch. Here he lived the rest of his life.

Dr. Hunt was a man of profound religious faith, a Baptist like the Morrises. He was matter-of-fact, yes or no; he said, "What you say, let that be it!" He wouldn't diddle with you at all; he didn't see any need of telling you a dozen times. I've heard him talk to patients over the telephone, saying, "Yes, I'll come," or "No, I don't believe I can get there." That's the way he was.

The date of original construction of Dr. Hunt's house, 1889, is visible here, as are the columns and wraparound porch added later. Photo by LLM.

He carried on his practice in the farming community in and around Gibson. Back then everyone traveled either on horseback or in a buggy or wagon. So it would take Dr. Hunt two to three, or even four hours to make a call down to Eldad and get back. But when I got to be six or eight years old, I would ride behind him on the horse, his medicine and equipment in bags slung across the saddle horn. (At that time he had long whiskers, down to his waist, and when he rode on the horse, they would flow back over his shoulders. Later in life, though, he cut his beard shorter, and in his last years he kept only a mustache.) I've also ridden many a time in the buggy with him; I've seen him lance a finger outdoors, the patient's hand resting on the buggy wheel, and Dr. Hunt using a pocketknife. He had good common sense and reason, and he had marked stamina, in spite of a hernia and hemorrhoids (they didn't operate on such things then), which he put up with all his life. I remember seeing him push his hernia back in and strap on an old ball truss. He took these troubles as a matter of course. He didn't *want* to change his way of living, and he didn't.

Dr. Hunt had four children. Two of them died in infancy and two lived, a boy and a girl. The girl, Bernice, became my mother; the boy was my uncle, Guy Hunt.

My grandmother, Lisa Hurt Hunt, died soon after giving birth to her last child, who died also. Guy and Bernice were still small when this happened, and Dr. Hunt took them to Milan to stay, I think, with Aunt Emma (Emma Robertson, his sister). Before very long, Dr. Hunt got married again, to Mrs. Mattie Scott of Memphis. This was during the yellow fever epidemic; a lot of people were sick and dying. Her father was a school-teacher—a principal, I think—who had been murdered. They always thought maybe he had expelled a boy from school; one night he was called to the door, and when he opened it, he was shot to death.

As soon as Grandpa married Mattie Scott, he brought Guy and Bernice back home, and Mattie helped raise them. I have a picture now of her in a buggy with Bernice. I often went over to their house, and always called her Grandmother. She died in 1924, during my first year of college.

Dr. Hunt stands near buggy in which sit Mattie Scott Hunt (his wife after Lisa Hurt Hunt died) and Bernice Hunt (his daughter). The handsome house he built in 1889 stands in the background. Notice the fence around the house, used to keep out animals that grazed on the lawn. Another fence bordered the lot on its perimeter. This reprint was given to Dr. Morris by his brother Guy in 1972.

Guy Hunt

After high school, Uncle Guy enrolled in Union University, the Baptist College in Jackson, Tennessee. When Dr. Hunt heard that his son wasn't attending classes, he confronted him: "Son, what's this I hear, that you're not going to school? I hear you're not going at times. Well I'll tell you one thing; I'm not paying for any such stuff like that. And if you *are* going to go to school, you can go on your own and borrow the money!" So Uncle Guy did that; he attended and graduated from a business school.

With his diploma, Guy went down to Baton Rouge, Louisiana, where his cousin Fanny Hunt Tucker lived. She was married and had two daughters, Docia and Erma. Guy Hunt lived in their home and got a bookkeeping job in a sugar refinery, keeping records of weights and other things. Later he became bookkeeper for the Louisiana state penitentiary, working under governors Parker, Fuquay, and Long. I remember seeing Uncle Guy twice: He came home on a visit after being away 30 years or so, then he came back one more time. Sometimes, Uncle Guy said, he would see Governor Long entering the capitol building, and would go in behind him, taking penitentiary vouchers for him to sign. But the clerks would tell Guy that the governor wasn't in. Uncle Guy told us, "Well, I knew good and well he was there, because I *saw* him go in!" It was Guy who gave Huey Long the nickname "Kingfish" that became so popular. The two men didn't like each other, and Guy either resigned or was fired from his position.[4]

The time came when Guy grew sick, and was in great pain. (My guess is that he had a ruptured ulcer.) The Tuckers persuaded him to go to the hospital. There, we were told, he hung his watch up on the nail over the bed and said, "All right, this is it!" And he died there.

Grandpa and my brother John went down to Baton Rouge and brought Uncle Guy's body back to Gibson. His funeral was held out on the lawn in front of Dr. Hunt's home, and he was buried in the Gibson cemetery, where today his tombstone gives the years of his birth and death: 1874 and 1933.

Grandpa Morris

I don't know much about my father's background. His father, John Peter Morris,[5] was kin to the Belews in some way; I don't know how. I do remember that he came up from Skullbone, Tennessee. He completed only the third grade of school, but his writing was neat and legible—better than mine. He did farm labor. He came down to Eldad[6] and was working for Dr. Hunt's brother, John Hunt, or for a Bass. I think he was converted to Christ down there. He married Sarah Chandler, George Chandler's sister, from Gibson. I have a picture of her. They had three children: Charlie, Mayme, and Joe (my father). At first they rented, living out from Gibson about two miles. Later, he bought a farm about two-and-a- half or three miles from Gibson, as you come around by the cemetery east of town. That's where he lived when I was a child. We took the gravel road in front of the cemetery, and it went to Grandpa Morris's place. I could also walk from our house or Dr. Hunt's through the fields two miles or so to get there. Sometimes I would go over to there on Saturday evening, spend the night, and on Sunday morning go to church with the Morrises in the surrey drawn by their two little mules, Jack and Kate.[7]

John Peter Morris (1852-1923) and Sarah Chandler Morris (1844-1897), parents of Joseph Edward Morris and grandparents of Dr. Robert Morris. This John Morris had only a third- grade education and farmed. He was a Baptist deacon, and some called him the "Peacemaker" because he helped settle disputes. Sarah Morris died before her grandson Robert was born.

Grandpa Morris worked hard, and was considered to be one of the strongest men in the community. He could take a barrel of flour and just lift it up on his shoulder and carry it and put it in the wagon. He was stout-built and strong, yet a very humble man, kind and gentle. Some called him "The Peacemaker" and would say, "John Morris can help you settle it." In the church and in the community, he would try to reconcile differences between people. And I have heard some say, "I wish I could be like John Morris," or, "I wish I could pray like John Morris." He was very religious. I never heard a smutty word out of his mouth. He served as deacon, and would be at church for every service—Sunday morning, Sunday night, Wednesday night, rain or shine.

Grandpa Morris had three or four horses and he sold some milk and butter and eggs. He had a little orchard and raised tomatoes, cotton, and corn —a pretty big job for one man. He was a wonderful watermelon grower. There was a tenant house on his land, but it wasn't always occupied. I can remember that one time a black man was killed in the community. They were searching for the one who did it and thought he had hidden in the empty shack on my grandfather Morris's place.

Grandpa could read but, as I have mentioned, he had only a third-grade education. When I'd go out there at night, I'd see him behind the stove, trying to read the Bible.

His was a godly home, as was my own. I didn't know anything else; this was the atmosphere I was raised in. My folks talked about Christ and Christianity all the time.

The former home of John Peter Morris. As a boy, Robert Morris often walked the two miles or so through woods and across fields to visit his grandfather. The farm was sold when John Morris retired to a two-acre lot across the street from his son Joe in Gibson. Photo 1989 by LLM.

The Freemans

By the time I was born, both my real grandmothers had died, and my grandfathers had both remarried. Papa's mother died when he was about 16 years old; they thought the cause was cancer of the stomach. I don't know how long it was after her death that Grandpa Morris married a widow, Mrs. Sarah (Sally) Freeman, whose maiden name was Nicholson. Before marrying Grandpa, Mrs. Freeman was living on one of the old roads between Gibson and Humboldt. She had two children, named Willie and Mable, from her first marriage. After marrying Grandpa Morris, Mrs. Sally gave birth to one child, Mildred (my Aunt Mildred, actually my half-aunt), who still lives in a retirement community outside of Denton, Texas, and is my oldest surviving Morris relative at 91.[8]

The combined Morris-Freeman family, after widower John Peter Morris (*center,
with beard*) married the widow Sally (Nicholson) Freeman Morris (*seated,
right*). The only child born after their marriage, Mildred Irene Morris, is between
them. Children from their earlier marriages are: (*standing*) Charlie Morris,
Mayme Morris (later Buckberry), Joseph Edward Morris, Mable Freeman (later
Luckey), and (*lower left*) Willie Freeman. If Mildred is three or four years old
here, the picture would have been taken in 1902 or 1903.

As Willie Freeman grew up, people at first thought he was going
to become a preacher, but instead he directed a boys' town for many
years in Nebraska, then moved to Louisiana. He married Ruby Hunt, a
relative of my Hunt grandparents; she was Zack Hunt's daughter and a
sister, I believe, to Joe Hunt. Willie and Ruby Freeman had W. T.[9] and
possibly other children. I never saw Uncle Willie again after he moved
away.

Aunt Mable married Will Luckey, son of John Luckey and brother
to Joe, Luther, and Clarence Luckey near Gibson. Will was recorder in
Jackson, Tennessee. He and Mable had two children. One of them died,
but the other one, Freeman Luckey, is practicing medicine in Florence,
Alabama, today, and his home is just around the curve from the home
of Melton and Trebor Ambrose. Aunt Mable, as a picture I have of her
shows, was a good-looking woman. After she died, Will Luckey married
one of her relatives, and from this marriage came two sons: David, who

graduated from Union University, but developed multiple sclerosis and lived in institutions until he died; and Hugh, who became a doctor—a cardiologist—and was superintendent of Cornell University Medical School, then later head of New York University Medical School. For all I know, he is living there in New York City now; his second marriage was to a Russian ballet dancer.

CHAPTER II
PAPA AND MAMA

In 1903, Joseph Morris and Bernice Hunt were wed in the parlor of Dr. Hunt's home. The bride was 27 or 28 years of age, six years older than the groom.

When Papa and Mama first married, they moved onto Grandpa Morris's farm and lived in a little log house on the hill north of Grandpa's house. Joe was thinking of buying a farm, but his father-in-law Dr. Hunt didn't want him to do that. He said, "You come and build you a home on my farm, and I will furnish you all the land you can work." So Papa did that; he built a little three-room house on Dr. Hunt's land facing the road, with a hall running straight through the middle, and with porches all across the front and back. This house was some 200 yards south of Dr. Hunt's house and is where I was born. They moved into this house the day of my birth, September 26, 1904. In fact, they didn't have time to get curtains up, so they just tacked quilts over the windows.

Dr. Hunt let Papa keep whatever he raised, and let him shelter his two head of stock in the barn. But Grandpa Hunt was this kind of man: He didn't want you going in debt, and he expected you to earn your own way; so Papa never borrowed much money from his father-in-law. There were two black tenant families on the Hunt farm, and we all used the same barn, feeding our stock out of different cribs but keeping our hay in the same loft. My father had to work hard for a living. He had no tenants and couldn't afford to hire help, so as soon as I was old enough, he *really* set me to work. Grandpa Hunt's tenants might help us put out tomatoes, and we'd help them cut hay.

The big barn was east of—almost directly behind—Dr. Hunt's house, the house where my brother Guy Morris lives now. One tenant house was behind the barn on a little hill; behind that house was the pond; and beyond the pond was the other tenant house.

Joseph Edward Morris (Sept. 3, 1881-July 19, 1967) and Bernice Hunt Morris (1875-1939), parents of Robert Hunt Morris, Evelyn Clair Morris, John Edward Morris, and Guy Franklin Morris. The couple was wed in 1903.

Ours was a peaceful home. My parents never argued. If Mama got upset, Papa would just cluck his tongue, "Tch, tch, tch. You ought not to do that!"

Papa

This is Papa's account of his conversion, as I remember him telling it: "I was going through the field one day; I was about 15 or 16 years old. Mr. Hardy Bass [our neighbor living on the street that passed our barn] met me and said, 'Joe, aren't you getting about old enough that you need a Savior?' That struck me, and I said in my heart, *I'll find Jesus if it's the last thing I do.*

"And so I went to searching. I'd go to the barn and pray; I'd go up to the mourners' bench at church, but still I wasn't getting satisfied. And finally, after going back and forth, praying and all, peace came to me. I got peace. From time to time after that, I'd worry about my experience:

Is there more? Is there more? But the Lord said to me, 'I've given you a crumb; build on it!' And I'm going to try to do that."

If ever one tried to live his faith, Papa did. I never heard a smutty word out of his mouth; just "Tch, tch, tch. Son, why did you do that?"[1]

Papa wasn't one to take offense. However, he related to me an incident that had occurred many years before in which he was strongly tempted to violence: He was a fruit inspector on the pack shed, and one of his friends, a Mr. Thorne, kept complaining that Papa was turning down too much of his produce. These complaints continued until, finally, Papa became so provoked that one day the thought hit him, *Well, I'll just cut his guts out.* But as he related this story to me, Papa said, "You know, it came to me: *Would I REALLY have done such a thing?*" In fact, he got so worried about it that he had to go and ask Mr. Thorne to forgive him for ever thinking such a thing. But as a result, he and Mr. Thorne were the best of friends until Thorne moved out of the community, and later died.

Papa had such faith that he'd sometimes say, "Well, quick as I die, I'm gonna see some beautiful things!" Sometimes he would go to men and talk to them about their salvation. I've seen him go to someone in church, put his arm around him, and talk to him, while I'd be thinking, *Lord-a-mercy! What are you doing?!* During a revival, if someone was bent over like he was under conviction, Papa would go to him and say, "Don't you think you need a Savior?"

An instance comes to mind that illustrates the spirit of my daddy: We were down cutting cabbage and it was hot. The old horse was grazing, trying to get some grass, and Daddy kept clucking to him, but he wouldn't bring his head up. Well, in Daddy's hand was the butcher knife he was using to cut cabbage, and he punched the horse in the side with the knife, not realizing he was hitting him with the blade rather than the butt of the handle . Then we looked around, and the horse was dropping blood; Daddy had cut two slits in his side. "Oooooooh!" Daddy moaned. "I wouldn't have done that for anything in this world!" "We pressed on the holes, and finally the blood stopped oozing, but Daddy kept saying, "I sure do hate that. I wouldn't do any person, much less an animal, that-a-way.[2] I'm so sorry!" We kept that old horse till he was 30 years old; he weighed 1400 pounds.

Papa worked hard—oh goodness! But he never made a lot of money. Besides farming, Daddy papered and painted. I went with him to a lot of homes, hauling ladders 'way out in the country when I was 14, 15, 16. I remember going over to John Lucky's, 'way beyond Antioch, and once to Mr. Meals' home, out on the road that is now between Three Way and Humboldt. Daddy also wrote insurance—some life, maybe, but mostly fire insurance on homes. For a while, he had an office downtown.[3]

Mama

My mother, Bernice ("Mama Bee" to my children), was of a meek and reserved temperament, more interested in home and children than anything else. Whenever I came home from school, I could count on her being there. All I had to do was holler, "Where are you, Mama?" and she'd say, "Here I am, Son." She was a good homemaker, and could take the little we had and make meals that were as good, to my taste, as any I've ever had. About the only groceries we'd buy were sugar, coffee, and flour; otherwise we raised our meat and grew our vegetables and fruit.

Mama was sweet and kind to us children, but she wasn't playful; she worked hard. Whenever she needed to, she would have me draw several buckets of water from the well, fill the washtub, and build a fire under it before going to school. Then she would take the old-fashioned washboard and scrub our clothes.[4]

She'd dress up and go to church with Papa, but I never heard her talk in public. Even at home she didn't lead in prayer or conduct devotions; that was Papa's role. But I'd see her reading the Bible by herself.

CHAPTER III
MY EARLIEST MEMORIES

The first dead man I ever saw was Rollie Hill. I remember Daddy carrying me in his arms to Rollie's home, and me looking at the body while he talked about Mr. Rollie, saying what a good man he was. I remember that Mr. Rollie had a little black mustache.

At Christmas time, when I was four to six years old, my father would carry us out in the hall, and he would say something like: "Santy Claus, bring 'em so-and-so," and we'd look up at the picture on the wall, waiting for an orange or apple to come down. I'd look around the picture to get whatever it was. We rarely got toys; one of the few toys I got was a tiny little wagon. I also remember getting a stopper gun with a breech to pump the air. I didn't get much else till I was 15 or 16, when Uncle Guy Hunt shipped me a bicycle from Louisiana, a Pathfinder. My daddy just didn't have the money to buy things like that.

When Christmas came, one of the tenant farmers would be sent over to get me, and he would carry me up to Dr. Hunt's house. Grandpa and Grandma slept on a feather bed. Now as a kid I had heard about "Santy Claus." I must have been seven or eight at the most. I'd spend the night there, and would have to lie there in the bed between my grandparents. I'd be anxious for morning to come, because I would hear them opening the closet, pulling out sacks. Well, it was just candy and nuts, and maybe an orange and an apple, but I was so excited I could hardly wait till day. I would get tired of being still and become restless, till Grandpa would say, "Boy, be still! I can't sleep!"; then I'd try to be still. Fortunately they rose early, and I'd get up as early as I could to see what I had gotten.

Uncle Guy Hunt would send pecans from Baton Rouge, Louisiana, and by the time I was eight or ten I would drive the buggy down to the depot by myself to get them. I remember that on one of these occasions, still before my teens, I hitched up old Clipper to the buggy and set off down the street toward the depot. On the way, I hit Clipper with the buggy whip. He kicked, and both his back hoofs shot up over the spatterboard and hung there. Since he was straining against his harness at the same time, he was unable to pull his legs forward and back down over the singletree. I had to get help and cut the harness loose to free him.

Robert, age five, stands in the gate while his mother, Bernice, holds baby sister Evelyn, in front of their home. Joe Morris built the house in 1904 and moved in with his wife the very day that she gave birth, later in the evening, to Robert, their first child. The photograph is printed on a postcard, which bears the postmark "GIBSON, TENN. / NOV 27 PM 1909." It is addressed to: "Mrs. W. D. Buckberry / Bowling Green, Ky." The message reads: "Hello Mayme / How are you. We are all well and getting along well. You must come hog killing time. I hate to send this through the mail. I am such a sight. / Bernice."

I remember when my sister Evelyn was a little girl, playing with her out on our porch, which by this time extended around the north end of the house. We had gotten a little tricycle for Christmas. I had her on this tricycle and pushed her off the porch, which was rather high. I reckon it just knocked the breath out of her, but I was scared; she looked so white and pale, I thought maybe I'd killed her. I said to myself, "Oh my goodness; I've killed my sister!"

The same house, seen here in a 1955 photograph, when it was occupied by Guy, Sue, and Frank Morris.

There was a low fence around the house, and I remember when the shade trees were first put out and were still small. There was a wire fence along the street, with (I think) a plank on the top and bottom, and a gate. I recall there being four to six shade trees, which are mostly gone now. Each tree was surrounded by a lattice to protect it until it could get some growth. I remember walking out to the gate with my mother one time, and her carrying Evelyn—I, a little boy, with my hat pulled back while they took our picture. I still have this picture.

I also remember having a picture taken over at Grandpa Hunt's on the front porch. I would go over to Grandpa's house and run upstairs and out on the little portico. I'd stand up there and think I was 'way up there. I'd slide down the banister, and think it the best ride I ever had. But the law was that I didn't go in the front bedroom, and especially not in the dresser drawers, unless Grandma was in there with me. The big wardrobe was off-limits, too; later I learned that she kept money in there. Grandpa had instructed her, "Spend a dollar; save a dollar."

I remember going in the barn and Daddy teaching me how to milk. Also, when I was seven or eight years old,[1] he tried to teach me to plow. Papa instructed me: "Son, just stop the team; lay the plow down; pull them around, and when they get stopped, raise your plow up, and then start 'em again."

County fairs were held annually in Humboldt, and included horse shows and racing. I would go with my grandfather, Dr. Hunt, because he was always interested in buggy horses and saddle horses. I especially enjoyed watching the races.

Robert Morris at perhaps six to eight years of age, on the porch of his grandfather Hunt's home.

When I was little, I didn't always want to go to church. Daddy would say, "Son, get on your clothes; you're going to go to church." And when we went, he was very strict about how I conducted myself. Back then, when people went to church, they didn't carry on idle conversation; they went to worship! When I'd squirm in my seat, Daddy would look back there, put his finger to his pursed lips, and whisper, "Be quiet! You're in the house of God!" If I made a racket, he would carry me out and say, "Listen, Son, I'm not going to carry you out any more!"— meaning that he would whip me next time. Church services were conducted differently than they are today; there was greater solemnity. Of course, after the service we would socialize a lot.

One day I was milking, and my little sister Evelyn came down to the barn wanting some milk. I said, "Well, Honey, you just open your mouth and I'll squirt some in there." So I squeezed the teat and aimed the stream of milk at her mouth, but it was hitting her all in the face. So I said, "Well, just take hold of it and suck it, then," and held the teat where she could get her mouth over it. But she bit down, and the cow jumped in surprise. One of her hoofs came down on the big toe of my right foot (I was barefoot, of course), and as the cow turned around to see what was going on, she screwed my toenail clean off. You ask did it hurt? What are you talking about! I went to the house screaming and crying; then for days they were telling me, "Don't get dew in it! You'll get dew poison!" My toenail did grow back, but so thick that to this day I have to trim it with a pocket knife; I can't get clippers on it.

CHAPTER IV

GROWING UP

Births and deaths

I was born in 1904, my sister Evelyn in 1909, then my two brothers: John in 1911, and Guy in 1917. I was around 13 when Guy was born, and when he started to school I was already finishing high school. Because of this age gap, I wasn't with him as much as I was with John and Evelyn, and we weren't as close until later years.

When I was seven or eight and John just a few months old, Mama developed a toxic goiter. She had a fast pulse, and tried to carry on her housework in spite of the growth on her neck, until we felt something had to be done. At that time, surgery was a rare thing—a last resort— but Dr. Johnson was performing surgery at the Baptist Hospital in Memphis, and Papa and Grandpa Hunt decided they'd better send Mama down there. Dr. Johnson said he knew how to cut but not how to treat a patient—that he'd get someone else to treat her, but he would operate. There weren't many surgeons then; he was one of the big names. Papa went with Mama on the train, carrying John, and was trying to feed him milk, buttermilk, and things like that by bottle. I remember Evelyn and me staying with our grandfather, Dr. Hunt. For a few days they were saying, "Your mother is seriously sick," and I would wonder, *Is Mama gonna die?* I don't know how long she stayed in the hospital, but they said, "Well, she's still living." Mama finally got well enough to come home, but Papa still had to tend to her and help her with housework till she got strong.

Ever after this, Mama would have occasional throat spasms: She would gasp and have striata of the throat, turning blue. At such times

I'd run over to get Grandpa Hunt, then maybe Mama would get over the spell. It is my guess that toxic goiter contributed to her eventual death.

Since we farmed land belonging to my Grandpa Hunt, shared the use of his barn and equipment, and lived so close, I considered his house my second home. When I was growing up, I ate as many breakfasts there as I did with my parents. Every morning and evening, I went through the vacant lot separating our two houses to milk at the barn behind Grandpa's house.

Death of John Peter Morris

Grandpa Morris, by the time he reached 68 or 69 years of age, was getting to where he couldn't work his farm. His family persuaded him to sell the farm and buy the little house and lot across the street from our house in the curve heading south out of town. Mr. Hollis Walker had built the house, and old man Stevens had first lived there. Uncle Charlie got Grandpa Morris to rent a little old store downtown and stock it with groceries, but the business lost money and Grandpa didn't stay in it long. After that, he and Mrs. Sally, my step-grandmother, just lived at home in retirement, with a little garden, one horse and a buggy, a cow, a hog, and his chickens. He had an acre or two on his little hillside.

In 1923, somewhere around my 19th birthday, Grandpa took the flu. My regular chores already included doing the milking at home and feeding the stock. Then, when Grandpa got down sick, Mrs. Sally had me milking the cow and feeding the horse for them, plus drawing water and slopping the hog. The family called for Aunt Mayme to come down from Bowling Green, Kentucky, to help Mrs. Sally in the house. But Aunt Mayme and Mrs. Sally both got sick, and so did Papa. Well, I was doing all the work at the two houses, and I think Grandpa had been sick about a week when, one day, I went back to his house to do some work and found him out drawing a bucket of water. I said, "Grandpa, what are you doing out, now? You don't need to be out!" He looked ashen pale, but said, "Well, Sonny, I think a little fresh air and exercise will help me."

I went on home, and soon Mrs. Sally called me and said, "Come back up here, Sonny. He wants to get on his clothes and go outside." I went back, and found Grandpa trying to put on his clothes. "Where do you want to go, Grandpa?" I asked. I've forgotten what he said, but we kept saying, "Grandpa, you can't get out. *Please* stay in bed." Finally he submitted and said, "Well, all right, I'll lay back down." He stayed there for a week or more in a stuporous, semi-conscious state, coughing up blood-streaked sputum; we knew it was pneumonia then. The only other thing he did was to pray, asking the Lord to take care of him: "Lord, direct me. Take care of me. Look after me. Forgive me of my sins"; and so on. I've never forgotten this. This continued until he died, perhaps 10 days after his illness began.

John Morris's body was put on display in his home. Papa was so sick he barely got across the street to see him, putting on an overcoat and sitting in the room, talking about him: Oh, what a father he'd been! Papa showed a great deal of emotion.

In those days, people lived in the home: They were born at home, were married in the home, were sick in the home, and died in the home. Home was the center of life. Now, it is anything but that. Too often today the woman is not in the home; she is in business or out working.

Work and play

Farm work was part of my everyday life from an early age, and there was no getting away from it. I've already mentioned that I learned to plow by the time I was eight years old. Milking the cow and feeding the animals were year-round, daily chores. A lot of the work was seasonal: planting, chopping, and harvesting. I took the hard work for granted, but was always glad for breaks. My sister and brothers worked on the farm too, but as the oldest son I was always doing the hardest jobs until I went away to college.[1]

We had a lot of tomatoes, and by the time I was 15 or 16, Papa occasionally would let me off work to go down to the pack shed and earn some money by nailing up crates. After others packed the crates, they'd turn them around on the bench and we'd nail on the tops. We'd get a ticket for each one, and they'd pay us so much for every hundred we nailed up. I've also helped load boxcars with produce to ship up north. Cabbage and tomatoes were shipped in ice boxcars on the L&N Railroad to St. Louis, Chicago, and other places.

In the early spring we tended our tomato and cabbage beds. We had a number of beds that had to be aired. We'd open them in the morning, then Papa wanted them closed up at two or three o'clock in the afternoon when it began to get cool. Our school had a 30-minute recess around two-something, and since Papa was often working away from the farm, and the school was so close to home, he'd want me to run and close up the tomato beds and then get back before the classes took up.

After school I had still other chores to do, but I wanted to play. A lot of mornings Papa would say, "As quick as school is out, I want you to come and help me dig potatoes"; or, "We're beginning to pick cotton now, and I want you to pick as much as you can before you have to do your milking and look after the stock." But I loved baseball and basketball, and would rather catch a fly ball than eat; so I would stay a while after school, usually playing ball. I've gotten many a whipping by not coming home on time. I'd see Papa coming across the school ground with a little switch, and he'd tap me on the legs all the way home. He'd say, "What did I tell you, Son?" I guess I would have been 10 or 12 years old at this time.

To play baseball, first we'd choose two captains, then one captain would take the bat and toss it upright to the other, who would catch it in his fist. They would alternate fist over fist until one of their fists covered the top of the bat, and that captain would choose first. We'd play after school, and I'd join them whenever I could.

The first basketball I ever saw was brought to Gibson school. We had heard of basketball but had never seen one and hadn't read the rules yet, so we just began bouncing this ball around on the ground in front of the high school. However, we did know that the game required a backboard and a rim to pitch the ball through. So we boys got someone to build us a backboard, and we went to the blacksmith shop and got the blacksmith to make us a rim with braces. Then some boys went to the woods and cut a long straight pole, debarked it, squared one side in its upper portion, and nailed the backboard onto it. By this time we also had game instructions, so we set the pole up at regulation height, and soon were ripping and romping out there, trying to pitch the ball in the goal.

Later we got to playing regular basketball on a court, and I enjoyed the game. Usually we just played at home, but I remember our going once in buggies from Gibson to Moore's Chapel to play against the Ing boys and some others from over there. Mr. Chun, our principal, went with us. It's the only time I remember playing out of town.

My dad wasn't in favor of our playing too much on Sunday afternoon as some did, and he warned me: "Don't go to this pond over there swimming on Sunday." We might play a while in our yard or a neighbor's yard, but would not go off to a field where others were playing in an organized way. They taught us back then: You don't work on Sunday, and you don't play and carry on on Sunday; it's a day of rest. Of course, we boys would go down to Robert Guy James', and we'd get to playing, maybe in his barn. One game we'd play was this: We had a rubber ball, and we'd lay our caps down. We didn't know whose cap the ball was going to be in. If the boy who was It dropped the ball in your cap, you had to pick up the ball and hit him before he got away. If you hit him, *you* were It and got to drop the ball. If you didn't ... well, I've forgotten what happened to you.

Robert Guy James was my age and lived across the street from us. His father, Mr. Nestor, was a banker and didn't farm; so Robert Guy would kid me because he'd be playing and would see me out there cutting stalks. I'd see him riding his bike, and I'd say, "Well, I declare! That's a sight to me, that I've got to do this every time I come home. I don't get no^2 time off." And when time came for our church business meeting, on the fourth or fifth Saturday, I had to go to church and sit there. I didn't care for all that business. They'd read the minutes, and discuss doing this and voting for that; then the preacher would preach for half an hour or more. I'd be sitting there, anxious to go to town, and when we'd get out it would be so late Papa would say, "Well, I don't expect you'd have time. You'd better go on home now. By the time you get home you'll have to go milk and feed."

"Hot" beds for plants were covered with sash (rectangles of glass in a wooden frame), and "cold" beds were covered with sheets. We'd plant cabbage seeds at Thanksgiving, and tomato seeds in January. We'd have to cover the beds with sash to make enough heat for the seeds to sprout. When they sprouted, we'd have to lift the sash in the daytime so the plants wouldn't overheat, then cover them again at night, stuffing straw under the sash to keep cold air out. When the plants were three or four inches high, we would transplant them to a cold frame, where we just had a sheet over the bed, plus straw if it got too cold. To make plant sets, we used dirt bands, which were grooved strips that we'd fold into square cups with about two- inch sides. The plants would be "hardened" by gradual exposure to cold to prepare them for planting.

We'd set out cabbage plants in February; tomatoes we'd put out around the 20th of April. Of course Papa worked with me in the field, and I'd go with him hauling ladders, but I wouldn't do the papering and painting. I might help him a little on his outside jobs, but mainly I had to do the work at home while he was out. I never got paid by my dad or knew anything about an allowance. If I wanted money I had to ask for it, unless I worked for someone else and earned it.

Close calls

One time we were hauling in animal fodder, which was lunch for our horses and mules. (At that time our fodder was the extra leaves of corn stalks, stripped off while they were still green. We would use one leaf to tie each handful, then bind an armful of the little bundles into a larger bundle.) It was already night time; we were working late because it looked like it was about to rain. I was 'way up on top of the wagon load, about 10 feet off the ground, when one of the bundles of fodder slipped and my foot gave way. I fell and hit the ground. Daddy thought it a wonder that I didn't break a bone, but amazingly, although it did knock the breath out of me, I wasn't really hurt at all.

Another incident involved my grandfather's buggy horse. Grandpa's stables filled most of a long shed running along one side of the barn, the rest of the shed being used to store plow tools. But one section was enclosed as a stall for the horse he used in his medical practice. One evening I was standing in the door of this horse's stall, just pitching corn into the trough about six or eight feet away from me, when a dog came around and barked. The horse snorted and bolted through the door, knocking me down and out cold. I really don't know what happened after that, except that I wasn't hurt to speak of. I said, *Well, there's another time I got by and it didn't kill me.*

One time our Sunday School class went on a picnic. We were sitting in the back of a truck that had high sideboards and a bench on each side. I'd guess the truck was going 30 or 35 miles an hour on the gravel road, and, like boys will do, some of the boys were picking and shoving, and grabbing each other's caps and throwing them off. I said, "Well, I'll tell you one thing. If you get my cap, I'll get it back. I'm not going to leave *my* cap down here." They took this as an invitation, of course; someone jerked my cap off and threw it out of the truck.

Well, without thinking how fast the truck was going, I hauled myself over the back end, thinking, *I'm gonna get my cap!* I hit the ground running, but couldn't run as fast as the truck. So I hit the gravel in a ball, and rolled and rolled and rolled. The truck came to a stop, and they were hollering, "I bet he's hurt now!" But I wasn't really injured, and I got my cap!

Entertainment

Often I'd say, "Papa, I want to go to town! I haven't been there this week!" I'd want to hang around and talk with the fellows, but he was always warning me: "I don't want you hanging around certain places"— certain places like the Central Office (the telephone exchange). The Central Office was upstairs. An old stairway went up there, and a lot of the rough boys of the town would get up there. They had a cage around this, and the fellow working the board was behind this cage. There would be a few chairs, and you could sit there. A lot of the boys would watch the operator work, while telling jokes and talking about women and girls; so Papa would tell me he didn't want me up there. A few times I went anyway, and got scolded for it. And if there was a dance or something, he'd say, "I don't want you down there."

There used to be a man who would come through in the fall showing silent movies. And I would beg Papa to go to the moving picture show, but he wasn't in favor of it. I guess I got to see one or two while I was growing up; he wouldn't let me have the money. He also didn't favor ice cream suppers and other fundraising activities of the church. He'd say, "I don't think it's the place for that, at the church. That's the place of worship, the house of prayer." He was like Dr. J. Vernon McGee who teaches on the radio, saying, "We've made the church more a pleasure house than anything else. There's more entertainment going on in church now than there is the gospel being preached. We talk about going over to the 'fellowship hall'; but over there you just fill your stomach, talk, and laugh a lot. True fellowship is around the blessed word of God."

Travis James' Sunday School class on a fishing trip in the early Twenties. *Left to right*, as identified by Dr. Morris: "Hassel [Haskell] Jones, John M. Dawson, _____Martin (?), Robert Morris,_____, J. L. Meals, J. C. Warmath, Morgan Warmath."

My nicknames

When I was growing up, most of the people around Gibson lived and worked on small farms. Jobs weren't available then like they are now, outside of the blacksmith shop, the bank, the grocery, and the barber shop—unless you got a job on the railroad as a section hand, freightman, flagman, or in the mail car. So I just wondered what I would do in life. I couldn't think of anything besides farming like my father or practicing medicine like my grandfather. I never felt inclined to become a banker or a teacher. Once when asked I said, "Well, I reckon I'll be a preacher." So they commenced to calling me "Preacher," and a few of my old friends living today, like Wayne Sadberry, still do.

The other nickname that stuck to me was "Rabbit." We would go down to the school ground and shave us off a round track with a hoe, maybe tying some cord to little stobs posted around the circle. We'd pair off to run; the one in front would be the horse and the one behind the driver. Each would be holding one end of a string in his hand, and we'd race around this track that we had made. I could run fast; they used to say of me: "By golly, he can really run!" That's why they started calling me Rabbit.

I was always a bit small compared to most other boys my age. By the age of 16 or 18 I was five feet seven-and-a-half or eight inches tall, and it seemed that I stopped growing.

School

Going through grammar school, I repeated the fifth grade. I had absolutely no idea what "invert the terms of the divisor and multiply" meant. Our teacher, for whatever reason, was unable to get this concept and others across to me. In fact, only one pupil, Jewel Davis, passed from my class into the next that year, and Mary Harris entered our class from the fourth grade. I guess it's a good thing I did get to repeat that grade; I sure didn't understand what I was supposed to learn. I had started school when I was nearly seven, so after repeating this grade, I graduated from high school in 1924 at the age of 19.

During my early school years, Gibson's only schoolhouse was a frame building with just two rooms—a big auditorium and one room on the side. Later they built a room on the other side, for a total of three rooms plus a porch. Then, about the time I entered high school, the frame building was torn down and a new brick building erected. (Several years after I graduated, a student burned this building down, and he spent three months in jail.) Mr. W. W. Chun was principal during my ninth-grade year (we called him "Willie Willie" behind his back); then Mr. J. A. Bobbitt came, and I finished high school under him.

I've had a lifelong fear of speaking in public, and this probably goes back to an experience I had in the ninth grade: Our high school had a debating society with monthly programs, and some of these debates would be open to the public. So one night, we were to debate about the love of Miles Standish and Sir Walter Raleigh for Priscilla Alden, and the school building was so full that people were sitting in the windows. Ruth Casey, Max Parker, and I were taking part, as well as others.

Robert Morris at age 19 and as a high school senior, in 1924 (notice what may be a class ring). Another photograph taken at this time shows him with calf exhibited for the 4-H Club.

When it was my turn to speak (I forget which side of the issue I was on, affirmative or negative), Mr. Chun called on me. I got up, and to this day I don't know what I said; I was befuddled and must have lost consciousness. All I know for sure is that Mr. Chun came and took me by the arm saying, "I expect it's time for you to sit down." "Well, all right," I said; but the audience was laughing, and I was so embarrassed that I said to myself, *This is the last time I'll speak in public.* (Later on, when I went to Union University and was invited to join a debating society, I immediately refused.)

At that time, in our community, people were saying you could get a little better training by going to Union, the Baptist college in Jackson; in fact, you could go there for your last year of high school and get your diploma there. J. L. Meals and Robert Guy James did that. But when I was in the twelfth grade, my parents didn't say anything about sending me to Union (they didn't have the money anyway); so there were eight girls and myself in my high school graduating class.

CHAPTER V

SIN AND SALVATION

Papa was very strict with me about going to school. He said, "Now, when you go to school, if you get a whipping—no teacher is going to whip you unless it's necessary, unless you've done something you shouldn't. And if he whips you, I'll whip you again when you get home."

The Dirty Dozen

Well, when I was in the ninth grade, about 16 years old, a group of local boys formed a gang they called the "Dirty Dozen." I'm sure it had been going on for a while before I knew anything about it. But one day they caught me, threw me down, and twisted my arm, saying, "Will you join the Dirty Dozen?" I finally said yes, and later twisted the arms of a few other boys to get them to join. But that was all I knew about the gang, and about my only real participation. I really didn't think much about it.

Now whereas I lived just across the street from the school, most of these boys were riding in wagons or buggies or else walking some distance to school. Apparently several of them did some mischief as they walked home along the railroad track—I never was sure what kind it was. But as a result, someone came to Mr. Chun, the principal, asking if he could get rid of the Dirty Dozen, and he replied, "Well, I'll see what I can do about it." So, during the Thanksgiving recess, while Papa and I were oiling the school floors, Mr. Chun walked into the building with what seemed like a whole nursery of peach-tree switches in his arms. I asked, "Mr. Chun, what are you going to do with all those?" He replied, "Well, you'll find out later." So I forgot about them.

But when school took up again after the holidays, Mr. Chun went around to each classroom, asking, "How many in here belong to the Dirty Dozen?" I raised my hand, along with the others, and he wrote our names down. Then he had Mrs. Lillian Hale vacate her room on the ground floor, and one by one he called us in there to see him.

When my turn came, and we were in the room alone together, he said, "Robert, do you belong to the Dirty Dozen?" I said, "Well, Mr. Chun, I really didn't know what was going on. I haven't been into anything. One day we were playing, and they caught me and got me down and twisted my arm and said, 'Will you join it?' And I said yes." Mr. Chun broke in: "That's where you stepped into it." I tried to defend myself: "Well, I hardly realized what I was getting into." "That's just the trouble. I wouldn't have thought that a boy trained in a home like the one you have, with the father you've got and the teaching he gives you, would do such a thing. But, on the basis of what I've said, I'm going to have to whip you."

So he whipped me, and I thought I was ready to leave until he said, "No, I'm not through with you; have a seat." And then he talked with me about my manhood and what I should try to accomplish in life. He reiterated what he had said about the home I was raised in, warning, "It will bring disgrace on your parents, if you live this way." Well, that talk hurt me more than the whipping I'd got. And of course Mr. Chun told my daddy that he'd whipped me, so Papa said, "All right, Son, I'll have to do what I said I'd do," and he whipped me again.

Sin leaves its mark

The railroad depot in Gibson was on the far side of the tracks, perched on an elevated bank eight or 10 feet high. The bank had been formed by excavating the ground beyond it, leaving a sizable hollow where water would collect. This pond would freeze over in winter, and boys would skate and play on the ice. Papa told me one day, "Son, I don't want you going down to the depot and playing around down there. Some of you boys are gonna get hurt!"

Old portion of downtown Gibson, facing the railroad. Photo 1989 by LLM.

But the boys talked about the fun they had ice-skating, and when I was downtown I heard them laughing and playing by the depot, so I thought, *Well, I just believe I'll go over there.* So I did, and there I found Robert Hill, J. L. Meals, Robert Guy James, and a few others—maybe Alton Manley— playing. I joined in the fun; we'd get a head start running down the bank, then skate across the little lake. Well, Robert Hill began aggravating J. L., stomping on his feet. J. L. warned him, "Now, if you don't let me alone, I'll knock you in the head with a brick or something!" But Robert Hill kept picking on J. L., so J. L. picked up a piece of coal and threw it at him. Robert Hill ducked, and that lump of coal hit me right in the center of my chin, splitting it open and leaving an inch-long furrow.

Oh, I thought, *I've got to go home now; my chin's bleeding, so Daddy's gonna whip me, because he told me not to go down there.* Woefully I trudged home, and when I got there Papa said, "Son, I *told* you! See what you got into for disobeying me?" Then Dr. Hunt took a clean handkerchief and covered the blade of his pocketknife with it. He raked the blade through my incision, trying to get the particles of coal out. Well, you could have heard me hollering a good distance; I yelled, "You're killing me! You're killing me!" But Grandpa kept saying, "I want to get as much of this coal out as I can." Then he pulled the skin together and strapped my chin.

The wound gradually healed, but the particles of coal that could not be removed created a faint black streak that was visible under the surface of my skin for at least 50 years.

Peanut penance

A group of us kids—Maurine Morgan, Mary Rozzell, Robert Guy James, J. L. Meals, and myself—were playing one Sunday afternoon. We were in Mr. Merce Fly's yard and looked in his smokehouse. It had an old door, fastened by a chain that ran through a hole in the wood. We saw a lot of peanuts in there, and Viola, his daughter, told us, "If you can get in there and get 'em, you can have 'em."

We were able to pull the door open about a foot at the bottom, so as I was the smallest in the group, the others held the door open while I crawled in and handed out peanuts to everybody. Well, I didn't think much about it, but at church that night, Mr. Merce went to my daddy and said, "I want you to get on your boy about stealing my peanuts."

When Daddy asked me about it, I said, "I didn't steal 'em! His daughter told us we could get 'em if we could get in there. They held the door at the bottom, and I got in and handed 'em out." But Daddy said, "That's not it. If he *feels* like you've stolen 'em, I want you to go up there and apologize to him, and tell him you're sorry for what you did." I said, "I hate to do that." "Well, you'll *have* to, Son."

So, reluctantly, I walked up the street to the Fly home and called him out: "Mr. Merce, I'm sorry that you feel like I stole your peanuts. But your daughter said that we could have 'em if we could get in. But if you feel like I stole 'em, I'm sorry, and ask you to forgive me."

Slack in discretion

During the First World War, we were at church on a Sunday morning. Our Sunday School class met out in the vestibule where the coats were hung. We boys were sitting there after the class ended but before the worship service began, and got to talking about how the government was asking people not to drive to church in order to conserve gasoline. Just then we saw Mr. Luther James driving up to the church in his car, so we said, "Now looka there; he's still driving *his* car!" Two of his grandsons, Robert Guy James and J. L. Meals, were in the class, and one of them said, "We ought to write 'He's a slacker' on his windshield." Alton Manley said, "Well, I've got a little yellow paint at home; we'll just put 'Slacker' on it. So he ran home and got the paint, while the boys discussed who would do it. I said I'd put one letter; so I painted a big capital 'S', and others put 'L-A-C-K', then a period. Then we went into the service, and I put the matter out of my mind.

I strolled home with my family after church, using the old plank walkway. We were passing Grandpa Hunt's house when Mr. Luther James drove by us in his car, and I saw him stopping in front of our house. *Uh-oh!* I said to myself. Irby Hearn, Mr. Luther's son who was lame in one leg, hobbled up into the yard and spoke to Papa: "Mr. Morris, come out here and look what your boy did to my car." After complying, and then letting the car drive off, Papa turned to me and asked, "Did you do it?" "Well, I was with the boys that did it, his grandsons and all. I put an 'S'; they put 'L-A-C-K'. I was in it that much." "I don't care what the others did. You were in it." Before you eat your dinner, you go to the barn, take out the horse, put the saddle on, and you ride out to where Mr. Luther James lives. And you call him out and apologize." "Oh, goodness!" "Either that, or Son, I'll whip you till you do!" "Well, all right, I'll do it."

So I went out there, some two-and-a-half or three miles to his house (later Travis James' home), where the roads cross between Medina and Gibson. I rode right up to the end of Mr. Luther's front porch and, without dismounting, called him out. I told him the part I had in it, and said, "My daddy said wasn't nothing for me to do but apologize. And I want to tell you that if you feel that-a-way about it, I want to apologize for it and want you to forgive me." Then I went home.

The old James house in 1989, with its original exterior intact. It belonged to
Luther James when the young Robert Morris had to ride his horse out and
apologize (which he did without dismounting) for an indiscreet act. Later,
Robert was baptized in the James' pond across the road from this house, which
stands at an intersection of roads between Medina and Gibson. The house was
later owned by Luther's son, Travis James, Robert's Sunday School teacher.
Photo by LLM.

I guess I did learn something from these incidents: They taught me
to be more careful about what I did.

Freight-train frolic

At some point in this same period of my life, Hollis
Miles, Merl Pitt, John Burns, and myself were hanging around together,
and the others began saying, "Let's catch a train and go to Humboldt."
Why, I had never dreamed of such a thing, but I went along with the
idea. My daddy was constantly warning me about the danger of catching
trains and the consequences if he caught me riding one. But somehow,
one Saturday evening, we caught a freight train when it stopped in
Gibson, and rode to Humboldt sitting up top of a full carload of coal.
We sat on big lumps of coal —which was a dangerous thing to do,
because if the coal had fallen off, we could have been killed. The train
slowed down just before entering town, and we jumped off.

We walked uptown, thinking we'd go to a picture show. I believe John Burns had our money, so he bought tickets, and got back five dollars more in change than he should have been given. *Well, we thought, we're doing all right!* When we got outside after the show it was about 11 p.m. and time to go home; we began discussing how we could get back to Gibson. I was already worried about my daddy finding out and what he would say and do when he did.

We thought about catching the 11:11 and "blinding it" (standing between two cars where we couldn't be seen), but someone said, "That passenger train doesn't stop in Gibson. It goes through there at high speed; we couldn't get off." However, a freight left shortly after the passenger train, so we decided to catch that. We thought it would slow down in Gibson, perhaps even stop to switch cars, and we could get off. But lo and behold, when we got up on Cedar Lane and looked out of the boxcar, waiting for a chance to jump off, the telephone poles were rushing by so fast that we said, "Well, looka there! Those things look like the teeth of a comb! And we can't get out here; we'll land on that pile of crossties and get killed!" So the train didn't stop in Gibson; instead, it continued on to Milan, seven or eight miles further down the line.

The weather was cool and damp as we pulled into Milan, and we were chilled. We walked until we noticed a man stoking the boiler for a building heating system; so we went into the boiler room to get warm. We told the man what we were doing, and he said, "Well, I'll tell you, boys: You'd better not let Sires, the police officer here, catch you. He will sure call your parents and get you home."

Well, that wouldn't do, so we crossed the street and snuck into the old hotel there. By now it was after midnight, getting close to one o'clock in the morning, and no one was at the desk. So we went upstairs and crept down the hall, trying to find a door that was unlocked. Soon we did find one, and went in. No one was in the bed, so we all got in it together, lying crossways. But before we could get to sleep, here came Erbie Harris (we called him "Slick") in the room, and he said, "What in the world are you boys doing here?" Thoroughly miserable by this time, I said, "I don't know, myself." "I'll tell you boys what you can do.

You can get out of here, and I'll take the room, and they'll never know anything about it." Speaking for everybody, I said, "We'll get!"

So we left the hotel. There were no more trains to catch, so we had to walk down the railroad track the entire distance to Gibson, in a cold drizzle, arriving home just before dawn, about 5 a.m. My heart was pounding; I imagined my daddy saying, "Robert, I never *dreamed* of you doing such a thing! Where have you been?!" I went to the back porch, pulled off my shoes, raised the kitchen window next to the cooking stove, and slowly crawled in. Then I eased the window back down, tiptoed to the door opening onto the stairs, quietly crept up to my room, and crawled into bed, hoping against hope that my daddy hadn't heard me. About half an hour later—six o'clock—he called me to get up and milk the cow. I said to myself, *Oh, goodness! I don't see how in the world I've got the strength to do it. I am so tired I don't know what to do!* I got up, milked that cow, and ate a little breakfast. Then Papa said, "Well, it's about time for Sunday School. You'd better take your bath and get ready now for church."

Well, all that time I was looking for him to say, "Where were you last night?" But he didn't say anything. *Well*, I thought, *he's just waiting to see what I'm going to say*. I also thought surely someone would tell him eventually and he would find out. Every day I expected him to bring it up: "Robert, what is this about you catching a freight train going to Humboldt, then Milan?" But the days stretched into weeks, then months, And he never said anything.

One day, when I was grown, I said, "Papa, I want to tell you one thing that I put over on you, and that I've regretted ever since." After hearing my story, he said, "Well, I don't know how that got by me." I said, "When you all went to bed, where did you think I was? Because you were always checking to see that all the children were in bed. And then you called me that morning and never said a word about it!"

But I can tell you one thing that incident taught me: I'd never put my hand on a boxcar out there today, to even *think* about catching it!

My conversion

My parents attended every church service and made us kids go too, but as a child I was never pressured into becoming a Christian. Still, my father being the type of man he was, I knew he was concerned about my soul. My first memory of thinking about the decision I would have to make goes back to one time when I was a little boy and happened to be sitting beside my step-grandmother, Mrs. Mattie Scott Hunt, on the arm of her chair. She put her arm around me saying, "I hope you'll become a Christian some day." Of course I would hear grownups talking about being born again, and would see people going up front in church to confess Jesus as their Lord and Savior.

When I was about 14 years old, I knew that pretty soon I would be approached about becoming a Christian, and Papa at one point said something like, "Son, I want to see you become a Christian; haven't you thought about it?" Well, one evening I happened to be thinking about this while milking the cow. And just then, looking down through the hall of the barn, I saw Bro. Adams, our pastor at that time, coming up the street and crossing the schoolground, heading in the direction of our home. *I betcha he's going to the house*, I said to myself. *They're going to say something to me, sure as the world! Well, it's going to happen. So the quicker I can get through milking and get to the house and get it over with, the better.*

Once finished with my milking and feeding, I carried the bucket of milk home, put it up, went in, and sure enough, Daddy said, "Son, we want to talk to you about becoming a Christian." "Well, all right." "Well, why don't you go on in the parlor? Bro. Adams is in there." *Just what I thought!* I said to myself.

So I went in the parlor, and they talked to me about it: "Son, don't you feel like you've ever sinned and done wrong?" "Oh, yeah." "Well, don't you know that when a person sins, he is separated from God if he stays in that state?" Then they read some Scriptures to me, and after praying, asked if I couldn't become a Christian, and I said yes.

Well, I did make a decision that evening, but it was two or three weeks later that I began to experience real repentance. I was plowing the field over by the woods, about a quarter mile from our house, when the Spirit of God began to deal with me about my sins. The one that troubled me most was stealing: *You took that 50-cent piece off your grandfather's mantle.* (I remembered getting it out of the little jar.) *Then you took seven cents out of the church money.* (Daddy was church treasurer, and once he had some of the money out; I saw a nickel and two pennies, and took them. Often I would ask Daddy for a nickel and he would say, "I don't have one." So I said, *I'm gonna get this nickel. And these two pennies ain't much.*) I hadn't thought much more about these incidents, until now they came before me and seemed so awful.

Remembering my deeds, and realizing how wicked they were, I got so miserable I felt like I would die. I felt like I couldn't keep plowing till night; I wanted to quit. About this time I heard the train whistle. It was the Number 104, which meant the time was around 3:30. "Oh goodness!" I said. "I've got two or three hours to go yet."

Somehow I managed to keep going, but I took out as early as I could, around six o'clock. When I got to the barn, there was my daddy. I said, "Papa, something has got to be done for me. I didn't get anything when you and Bro. Adams talked to me. Something's gotta be done, or I'm going crazy!" Papa, who was never loud or hurried in speech, said, "Well, what's the matter, Son?" I said, "I don't know. Listen, I'm the meanest person in the world!" "Well," he said, "I'll be glad to talk to you about it. Take your team out, water it, feed it, milk your cow, and come to the house, and I'll talk to you." "All right, sir," I said.

As quick as I could I got through these chores. I went to the house, put the milk up, and Papa came out in the yard so we could talk by the woodpile. He said, "What is it, Son, that you want to talk about?" "I don't know. I feel so burdened—stealing, and everything else. I didn't get anything the other day." "Well now, Son, I wish I could do something for you. But you're in a state where I *cannot* do anything for you. But I can tell you One who *can*. If you'll just put your faith and trust in Jesus, He'll save you." Papa's words helped me, and I prayed this way: "Lord Jesus, I'll trust you, if it's the last thing I do!" And the burden left me.

After that talk with my dad, I presented myself as a candidate for baptism and church membership. We held all our baptisms at the big pond across the road from Luther James' home, and there was a big line of us when I got baptized. I remember being up on the bank and singing. I didn't fully realize what I was doing, but I do remember being in that pond, and Bro. Adams baptizing me.

All through my life, from time to time doubts have arisen as to whether I have really been saved. But I look back to that experience and say, "I know something happened there." Also, although I can't explain this, I have felt God's assurance, and this has given me a measure of peace. I know Paul said, "Forgetting those things that are behind, I press forward."[1]

CHAPTER VI
GIBSON BAPTIST CHURCH

The old building

My earliest memory is of a white frame building. It faced west, whereas the present building faces north, and was surrounded by a wire fence with a board running along the bottom, then a narrow plank on top stretching from post to post. We boys liked to walk along the top plank. I don't remember too much about the worship in that building. But I do hazily remember going to another white church building down the street while they were tearing our frame building down and Mr. Luther James was building a big new brick one. This first brick building, facing in the same direction as the frame building before it, burned in 1942.[1] It was replaced by the present brick structure facing Highway 79. When this second brick building went up, Highway 79 had just been completed.

The first brick building

I would guess that this building was able to hold 300 to 400 people, or even more—a good size in that day. It was said to have the best acoustics in the county. Behind the platform, which supported the pulpit and the choir, were four Sunday School rooms, while at the front of the building on either side was a vestibule where attenders left their coats, hats, and umbrellas. Between these two vestibules were two large Sunday School rooms, divided by a movable partition so they could be converted into one large meeting room. This room is where our business meeting was held on the last Saturday of each month.[2]

Gibson Baptist Church's first brick building, constructed during Robert Morris's youth by Luther James. Dr. Morris remembered it as having a capacity of 300-400 persons and excellent acoustics. Photo supplied by Sue Morris.

When I was in high school, I was the janitor for the church; I'd make $5 or $10 a month cleaning and firing the coal furnace—that was pretty good money then! I'd have to go down on Saturday evening to fire up the main furnace, then again about 5 a.m. on Sunday morning to light the stove in the big Sunday School room.[3]

The people

Most fellowshipping was done outside the building. The men —men like my two grandfathers, Dr. R. H. Hunt and John Peter Morris— collected under the big oak tree in the yard, shaking hands and saying, "Hello, brothers. How are you?" But inside the building, we maintained a solemnity, more so than I see in churches today. If we greeted someone, it was in a low tone—we came to worship, not to socialize.

We had a piano and a nice choir. Mrs. Mary Dawson was our pianist for many years. (She taught piano to me as well as to my children Una, Trebor, and Robert, some 35 and 40 years later!)[4] We had some good voices in the choir: Mrs. Kate Scruggs, Herman Mathis, Joe Hunt, Mr.

Nestor James, Dr. Rozzell, the Warmath girls, Ruby Warmath, and the twin Hazelwood girls, come to mind. Mrs. Scruggs and Joe Hunt were fine soloists.

Present building of Gibson Baptist Church, constructed after earlier building burned down in 1942. Photo by LLM, 1989.

The First Baptist Church of Gibson drew its strength in large part from a core of devout and dependable men—deacons such as Luther James, Ed James, both of my grandfathers (John Morris and Dr. Hunt), Dr. Rozzell, Nestor James, Calvin Warmath, and my father Joe Morris. Ours was one of the strongest small-town churches in Gibson County.

The preaching

The church did not have a parsonage nor a full-time pastor back then. One of the earliest preachers I can remember is I. N. Penick, who later taught me Bible at Union University. On Saturday afternoons, Bro. Penick would take the train from Jackson to Humboldt. There my daddy and I would pick him up, after driving our buggy over seven or eight miles of dirt roads to get him, and he might stay at our house overnight before preaching on Sunday morning.

Another preacher we had was J. E. Skinner, whose son also preached for us later. And I can remember Bro. Puckett; the church built its first parsonage for him. This house, built by Travis and Luther James, was well constructed and still stands. It is the second house up from my brother Guy's, but is no longer owned by the church. Today the church has a brick parsonage adjacent to the sanctuary itself.

I heard many a sermon on hell. They made such an impression on me that it seemed to be constantly on my mind, even outside of church. I might be watching my daddy and other men digging a grave for a friend or for someone who couldn't afford to pay a grave-digger, and I'd think, *I wonder if this fellow went to hell? It would be awful if he was in hell burning up!" I was taught that hell is something terrible—a place of fire, weeping and wailing, gnashing of teeth, outer darkness, no rest day or night, forever!*

Then too, I heard many sermons on being born again. The men I heard were continually preaching Christ, like Paul who said, "I purposed not to know anything among you save Jesus Christ, and him crucified."[5] They taught what Christ did for us: He bore our sins and was raised to justify us. That was drilled into me.

Other aspects

We were taught not only about salvation, but also to obey God's commandments, for: "If you love me, you will keep my commandments."[6] And we were taught to care for one another. Announcements were regularly made about those in the community who needed help. For instance, if someone's home burned down, we would get him clothes, find him a place to live, perhaps have a special collection. If a farmer was sick and unable to work his crops, we would meet and work out his crop together—plowing, hoeing, or harvesting. My daddy practiced private charity, too: He'd say, "I'm going to take this down to so-and-so, because I feel like they need it." He might take kindling wood, shingles, garden vegetables, or something else to eat.

For a long time, there were only two churches in Gibson—the Methodist and the Baptist. Later a Pentecostal church was established, way out in the country on the Trenton road at New Enterprise. Baptist beliefs were distinct from Methodists. We emphasized the new birth, and practiced only the ordinances of water baptism (for believers, therefore not for infants), and the Lord's Supper. My daddy warned me many times that salvation is a matter of the heart; that the act of baptism can't save, but that a person who has come to salvation *ought* to be baptized, because it demonstrates his faith and pictures the death, burial, and resurrection of Christ.

The Lord's Supper was offered once or twice a year in special services that were very solemn occasions. We did not feel bound to a particular schedule ("as *oft* as ye partake"[7]), but considered that the Jewish Passover was held once a year, and now Christ is *our* Passover. Usually the passage from I Corinthians 11 was read. The preacher would come down to the table and make a few remarks, and he would call on someone to lead us in prayer over the bread, then later over the juice or wine.[8] The only sound heard as the bread was passed would be the snapping off of pieces of unleavened bread. After taking the elements, we would sing a hymn, then walk out.

Revivals

We generally had a revival in the fall when the weather began to cool and farmers had less work. The church would bring in a revivalist or a preacher that we thought to be especially effective. The meetings normally lasted a week, going from one Sunday to the next. There was little entertainment in our community, so revivals attracted the unchurched and well as churchgoers. Young people would come; it would be a community event. Back then, it wasn't unusual at all to hear shouting. I can remember Mrs. Rose Manley and Mattie Chandler going up and down the aisle, shouting and praising God for what He had done for them.

We didn't rifle people out to pressure them into a profession of faith. However, if my daddy or someone else saw a person who appeared to be under conviction or considering a decision, they might go to him, put their arm around him, and speak to him. Occasionally, too, Papa would be concerned about an individual in the community and go to see him to talk about the Lord.

Religion in our home

We didn't have regular family Bible reading or devotions, but Papa got us kids to read our Sunday School lessons, and he himself read the Bible a lot. At times I could see my father come in the kitchen and wash his face, but not join us to eat, and I'd say, "Papa, what's the matter with you?" He'd say something about 'fasting.' "What do you mean? Why aren't you eating?" "Well, there's something on my heart." Usually he would miss all his meals that day, then come to the table the next. Fasting was something I never heard about in church and have never tried, myself.

CHAPTER VII

COLLEGE, AND FIRST ATTEMPTS AT MEDICAL SCHOOL

Union University

I had made up my mind that I'd be a doctor, so I went to Union University in Jackson, about 20 miles from Gibson. (Union is supported by the Tennessee Baptist Convention [Southern Baptist].) However, I had been at Union only a few weeks when I got homesick, thinking I had a better life at home than at college. I had such a lovely home and was so close to my people that I really didn't want to get away. I was just caught up with working at home; being the oldest child, and my dad needing someone to help, naturally I was used to hard work from a young age.

The problem for me at Union wasn't so much the work itself as it was the social atmosphere, in which I felt uncomfortable, and the academic competition from some of the other students who were bright and had graduated from better high schools. For example, I had never had chemistry, and some of them had. I had never learned to mix and mingle with strangers; I only felt comfortable with the boys I had known all my life. I had always stayed around Gibson, and was 16 or 18 before I ever saw Memphis. As best I can remember, I was 15 or 16 when I first visited Jackson, going there to spend the night with Hubert Cannon. Humboldt, Milan, and Trenton were really the only towns I knew besides Gibson. I wasn't accustomed to the larger world, and felt I'd rather go back home and plow than stay at Union.

So I called my daddy and told him, "Papa, I don't believe I want to go to college. I believe I prefer to stay at home and work like I've been doing; I've enjoyed it." "Noooooo, you're not! Son, I've paid your tuition for a year, and you're not *about* to come home until this year is up. I've *paid* for it!" "Well, I guess I'll have to stay here, then."

I attended Union University from the fall of '24 through the spring of '27, spending summers at home. (Professor Waters was president at this point.) Mattie Scott Hunt, my step-grandmother, died during the first year, so I went home for her funeral. But I remember very distinctly that, when I got back to Union and first entered my French class, old Dr. Savage (a former president of the school) said, "Morris, where have you been?" "I went home to my grandmother's funeral." "Let the dead bury the dead! This should be your work!" *What in the world did he mean by that?* I thought. But he was that kind of a fellow; he said, "They're dead and gone; go about your work."

In spite of difficulty adjusting to life at Union, I can see now that I did receive spiritual nourishment there. For example, A. W. Prince, my chemistry professor, was a prince of a fellow. Years later I noticed a few editorials that he wrote for the Tennessee *Baptist and Reflector*. He was matter-of-fact, thorough, and tough; the University of Tennessee was eager to have students to whom he had taught chemistry. And Dr. Savage, mentioned above, was a man I admired as being well-organized. He was a stickler for doing things on time. In chapel, he'd take his watch off and say, "I can leave this auditorium and be at my office upstairs in 60 seconds. And you ought to leave here just like water flowing down the River Jordan. You ought to get ready for your work." He filled his time; he didn't waste it.

Union had daily chapel services. Each seat had a number; one was assigned to you, and you had to occupy that seat. Someone marked down the numbers of the unoccupied seats as a way of recording absences. And you had to attend a certain percentage of the services or you couldn't graduate. (Today Union still requires students to attend a certain percentage of the chapel services. I see the students being handed cards that they drop into a box as they leave chapel.) Usually, in chapel, someone read the Bible and made a few remarks. Dr. Dunn, our physics professor, might say something. Dr. C. W. Davis, professor of zoology and botany, might have different plants on the platform to illustrate his talk. Once he talked on evergreens and drew a lesson from them.

At Union I took Bible under Dr. I. N. Penick, who had been one of our pastors in Gibson. When I first saw him there, I said, "Well, here's Brother Penick!"

So I went to Union for three years. I didn't get the bachelor's degree, because medical school would accept you then after three years of college (sometimes after only two, I think). So I entered U.T. School of Medicine in Memphis in the fall of 1927.

First attempts at medical school

Well, I went to Memphis, enrolled, and found it to be a bigger transition than anything I'd ever experienced. I had taken courses in zoology, botany, and chemistry, but some students were better prepared for anatomy than I. Then, too, the atmosphere at U.T. was different from that of Union, and the beliefs of the U.T. teachers were different from the beliefs of my Union professors. I heard some teachers saying things I'd never heard before, using foul language and expressing views foreign to my Christian background.[1] Too, I had never touched a dead body, as far as I know, until I went to medical school. And finally, I was farther away from home than I had ever been before; I had been to Memphis only once before, with Sam Scruggs, the Gibson druggist.

My first hurdle in Memphis was to find room and board in a home—a strange home. Next, I had heard stories of medical school, and some had told me, "It's terrible!" All these feelings and thoughts piled up on me. Then I went to get my box of bones (a complete skeleton minus one arm and one leg) and attended my first anatomy class. Those anatomy terms—I had never heard of such words, and I couldn't pronounce them. There were either 127 or 129 students in the class. The professor would march up and down this long room, spitting out words that I couldn't write down, much less spell correctly; I was never so lost and confused in my life! Other students told me, "You'll get in line after a while; you'll hear them so much that it will become a part of you." But I studied that stuff—what are you talking about!— trying to get straightened out in anatomy.

Then they took me down to the bottom floor of the anatomy building. I turned to my left and entered this room with three or four large vats, each one about two feet deep, with a big lid and a pulley on it—I reckon to bring the lid up. Several bodies were floating in each vat; the employee would use a hook to pull them out. Then around the room were shelves with other dead bodies on them, and a machine pumping this embalming fluid into them. (They embalmed them in such a way as to precipitate the fat off, and put a dye in the arteries. The body would blow up like it was going to burst, then, after the fat had precipitated, the body would settle back down and become firm. This process would preserve the bodies—I don't know how long, but a long time—then they were transferred to the vats to keep the skin from getting dry and hard. There were both whites and blacks, but more blacks, I believe.) Well, when I saw these vats with bodies floating around in them, I said, "Lord have mercy! I've never touched a dead body in my life, and you mean to tell me, mister, I've got to handle those things?" I thought I was going to croak!

The boys with me were from Mississippi, Alabama, and all over: New York, Chicago, Arkansas. Some of those from New York were shrewd; they had had a lot of premedical training. Some from Mississippi had taken their first two years of medical training in their home state, then transferred to U.T. for their last two years.

But I exhausted myself trying to keep up with classes, and became nervous and mentally fatigued to the point that I couldn't sleep. When I tried to rest at night, I would be naming the muscles, over and over. So after about three months, at the end of the first quarter, I withdrew without taking all of my tests.

I stayed home nine months, but in the fall of '28 I reentered and did nearly the same thing. And that's when Dr. Wittenborg, my anatomy professor, said, "Morris, if you'll stay on and settle down, I'll pass you without an examination; I'll see that you get by." I said, "Dr. Wittenborg, I'll tell you the honest truth. I *can't* settle down; I'm worried to death. I can't sleep, can't rest; I've just studied and studied and studied until I can't relax. I just can't take it any more!"

Papa's prayer

So, I went back home again. And my daddy said, "Well, if you don't see that you like medicine and can go through with it, and if you want to farm, well then get ready, because you're soon going to have to plant tomatoes." This time I stayed out of school nearly three years. I started out fixing my tomato beds, helping the blacks over there on Grandpa's farm to rive out (split) tomato stakes, clean out the stables, and haul manure. You can imagine the shape I was in, with my state of mind and doing that hard work: I felt like I had failed; I had spent all that money and knew how hard it was for my family to send me to school.

Because I was so nervous and upset, Daddy carried me over to see Dr. George Penn in Humboldt. (It was Dr. Penn who later gave me a steel box for obstetrical instruments that I have to this day. His brother, Ben Penn, was a good Christian man, and George used to say, "Well, if you want a *doctor*, call me, and if you want a *good man*, call my brother.") Dr. Penn gave me some potassium bromide just to quiet my nerves, and said, "Well, Robert, let me tell you something: One time I got sick, and I took some medicine, Calomel, and I passed so much from my bowels that I thought I had passed the bowel lining too. *Well,* I thought, *this is gonna kill me!* So I got up on the clothes box and folded my arms to die. And do you know what? I didn't die! And do you know what I did? I said, 'I'll never die again till my time comes!'"

Dr. Penn was tough as a whale bone; for instance he would perform an appendectomy in the home. I don't think his words encouraged me much, given the state I was in, but I haven't forgotten them.

When I wasn't planting or harvesting, I worked for Brown Parker, hauling ice, coal, and gravel in the summer and fall. I was driving a dump truck and an ice truck. Hauling ice was hard work for 35 cents an hour, but gradually my health returned and I got back into pretty good physical shape. About this time, I overheard my daddy praying a prayer that I've never forgotten: "Lord, I've tried to raise that boy the best I know how. And if he goes crazy, I'll accept it. But if You would take him and make something out of him, I will thank You. I leave him in Your hands."

Well, I don't know whether Papa's prayer worked on me right then, but I often thought about it during those three years at home. I believe the Lord put me in a position where I had to make a decision. Either I was going to farm all my life or not; and if I *was* going to do something else, I'd better get started doing it. One year, I had 4500 tomato plants up there beside the woods, and a field of some of the finest cabbages I've ever seen, but I had to work like thunder just to cover my expenses. However, I can say this: I knew how to plow and how to work a field about as well as anybody.

But as I plowed and as I hauled ice, the question kept haunting me: *Is THIS what I'm going to do in life? Is THIS what I'm going to do the REST of my life?* And then I would tell myself, *Well, I don't know anything else I want to do except practice medicine.* Still, it bothered me to think that I'd already been to medical school twice, and that I might go back down there and run into the same problem again. If that happened, I'd go nuts sure enough! Still, I had to make a decision, and certainly didn't want to haul ice the rest of my life. I knew that ordinarily they didn't let a dropout back in medical school, but one day I just said, "Papa, I believe I'll go back to medical school, if I can get in." "What?!" "I believe I'll go back to medical school." Dr. Hunt and others in the family said, "You are?" "Well, yes, I thought I would try it if I can get in."

Accepted

So now we had to drive to Memphis, where I went to see Dr. Hyman, dean of the medical school. As I entered the door of his office, he said, "Morris! Are you back here?" I said, "Yes, sir, Dr. Hyman, I've decided that if I can get in medical school again, I'd like to try it once more." He replied, "I don't commonly do this. This is not my way of doing business. But I feel that when you were here before, you showed that you had the ability, but you just didn't know how to be considerate, and that you can't learn everything in a day. It takes time; you've got to pace yourself; you've got to be consistent in your study, and in time you will learn it." This encouraged me to continue: "Well, I just can't get it off my mind. I'd like to go again." Dr. Hyman considered the matter for a while, asking more questions, and finally announced: "Well, I'm going to let you try it once more." "Dr. Hyman, I sure would appreciate it." "Well, all right; you can enter this fall."

After telling the news back home, we returned to Memphis to find a room I could live in. I found one, a block and a half above the medical school on the north side of Madison Avenue, with Mrs. A. K. Ash.

Memphis General Hospital was down the hill from me, with Baptist Hospital and Campbell's Clinic facing it on the other side of Madison. The medical school was behind Baptist Hospital on Monroe, and Eve and Lindsey Halls, used for lectures and outpatient treatment, were sandwiched between Baptist and Campbell. Eve Hall was named for the Dr. Eve who had been one of my grandfather Hunt's medical teachers in Nashville before the U.T. School of Medicine was even established.

This was in the fall of '31. After making arrangements for my room, I went down to the anatomy building to get my box of bones. I had to go up to the fifth floor (the lower floors were for physiology, neurology, organology, embryology, and chemistry), because skylights in the roof gave the top floor better light for dissecting. As soon as I planted my feet on that last step, about 40 feet from the door of Dr. Wittenborg's office, Wittenborg spied me and boomed out: "Morris, with your alligator shoes on! Are you going to enter this institution again?" "Well, Doctor," I said sheepishly, "I *wanted* to; I *thought* I would." "Well, all right, if that's what you want to do!" So now, for the third time, I was in medical school.

CHAPTER VIII

COMPLETING MEDICAL SCHOOL

The fall quarter had not progressed very far when anxiety began gnawing at me just as it had in my two previous attempts at medical school. Was this feeling going to grow until I was unable to function, like before? Even though I knew exactly what I was going to have to do—dissection, chemistry, neurology, organology, and embryology—I felt like I just couldn't do it.

But in spite of these feelings of failure, I somehow kept going on. I believe the Lord answered Daddy's prayer by putting me in a position where I either had to keep going or lose everything. So I gritted my teeth and said, *Well, I'm going through this medical school, and if I don't get through it, I'm going back home in a coffin!* I was *not* going to go back home a third time and tell them I had quit! So when that old feeling would come up again, I'd say to myself, Noooope, I'm going to stay HERE! And the anxiety would wear off in a little while.

Then, when grades for the first quarter were announced, I was leading my class, and I did so again the second, third, fourth, fifth, and sixth quarters. I began feeling better and better and getting bolder and bolder. However, I didn't get along so well with Dr. McElroy, the professor of medicine. He was brilliant—a no-nonsense type, rough on students, from Hushpuckena, Mississippi. He gave me a "B" in seventh-quarter medicine, which threw me back to seventh place in my group. This made me work extra hard the last five quarters, and I finished medical school third in overall grade average.

Another motivating factor was that only the top three students were given internships at Memphis General Hospital, and I wanted one because I knew I would get the best training there. Since only one intern was admitted to their program each month, and I was third in my graduating class, I had to wait two months to begin my internship. Ahead of me were Spruel in first place and Leo Harris in second place.

The April 1934 graduating class, University of Tennessee School of Medicine in Memphis. Dr. Morris is third from left in front row.

Graduation

I officially became *Doctor* Morris in April 1934. Graduation exercises were held in the medical school library, sandwiched between the anatomy building and the dental school. The three buildings were connected together; you could walk through the complex all the way from Monroe Avenue to Union Avenue. Unfortunately, a heavy downpour on graduation day kept my family from attending; in fact, the only "home" folk there was Mr. O. P. Parker, who had been reared in Gibson but now was head of a drama enterprise, writing plays for high schools. It was he who had brought me the news when J. L. Meals was killed and Robert Guy James seriously injured in a car accident. Also present that day, but unknown to me at the time, was my future fiancee, Lillie May Leake, then a U.T. student nurse.

The keynote speaker for the commencement was an old federal judge surnamed Martin. I still remember one thing he said to us that day: "You doctors are the biggest suckers for stocks, as a group, that I ever knew."

CHAPTER IX

INTERNSHIP AND ROMANCE

I was eager to begin my internship, the last major phase of my medical training, but had to wait two months before starting. After a short visit home, I returned to Memphis early—in May 1934, I believe—and began to do some relief work in the emergency room.

Here is my schedule of internship rotations, to the best of my recollection:

2 months in the Receiving Ward (Emergency);

4 months in Medicine, rotating through the wards—White Men, White Women, Colored Men, Colored Women;

1month in Pediatrics;

2months in Obstetrics ("OB");

3 months in Neurology;

2 months in Isolation;

6 months in General Surgery, including 1 month in Neurology; 3 months in Gynecology ("GYN").

So, including the first two months where I volunteered for Emergency, I spent a total of 20 months in my internship.

The Emergency Room rotation at that time normally came at the end of the internship. Emergency wasn't popular with the interns; in fact some of them avoided it by skipping out as soon as they had finished their stint in Surgery. They would say, "I've done got what I want: I've got my training in Surgery and I've gone through Medicine, Isolation, Pediatrics, through OB —I'm not *about* to do that Emergency!" So they'd just quit and go to practicing. Then Dr. McElroy, the medical school dean, said, "Well, I'll fix that! I'll put Emergency Room in the *middle* of your internship." However, when I got in the middle of my internship and ready to leave Surgery, they gave us a week or two of vacation. When I came back from vacation to go on Gynecology, why, they had stuck the Emergency rotation in before Surgery! So Dr. McElroy told me, "Well, you'll just have to stay on Surgery"; whereas the others had to go to the Emergency Room. So I stayed on Surgery an entire year, including OB, Neurology, GYN, and General Surgery or operating room.

As interns, we received $20 per month plus room and board—just enough for socks, cigarettes, and maybe one picture show a month. (In contrast, today's interns are paid several thousand dollars a month.) We were housed in the Como building, between the hospital and the old fire station. The fire station stood in the corner of the block that had been taken over by the City of Memphis, and on which the new John Gaston Hospital was being built.

If you want to know about long, hard hours—well, that was internship. We didn't have regular shifts; we were on call 24 hours a day, seven days a week, unless we got someone to relieve us. We were summoned by a bell system; my ring was two longs and a short: "Dooooong, dooooong, dong." I'd say, "There's another one!"

Rotation in Medicine

When I began my rotations in July 1934, the weather was hot. Heat stroke victims with temperatures of from 105° to 108° were being brought in, their thermal centers knocked out. Others were being brought in: some in a malarial coma, some with typhoid encephalitis, and one with sepsis (systemic infection), contracted from a piece of steel in his little finger. Up to this time I had taken histories but had never been responsible for diagnosing and treating patients. I had never written a prescription. My supervising resident in Medicine was Dr. McNabb, so I phoned him: "Dr. McNabb, come over here. If you don't, they're going to die like flies." He replied, "When you've been here as long as I have, it'll not worry you a lot. Do the best you can."

Hanging up, I thought, "My goodness, what am I to do?" So I began asking the nurse how they treated these cases. For a heat stroke patient she said, "We'll just have to get him in the bathtub, pack ice around him, and try to get his temperature down." We'd do that, and when his temperature had dropped to 104° or 103°, we'd put him in bed, dampen the sheet, and turn the oscillating fan on him—there was no air-conditioning then!

The chief of medicine in Campbell's Clinic, Dr. Hamilton, was also general supervisor of medical wards. So I asked if he would come help me. He was a kind man and a member of the First Baptist Church in Memphis. He came and advised me on heat stroke: "Well, these kind of cases commonly go into heart failure." But we began digitalizing them and saved two patients, although two or three others died of congestive heart failure. If we suspected malaria, we'd take a blood sample, run it, and find out if the patient had this disease. We treated malaria patients by reducing their fever and by giving them Atebrin, which was a replacement for quinine; we were keeping a record to see how well Atebrin did in malaria. We had a few cases of diabetic coma; I had had no previous experience with this. The patients would get acidosis and go into a coma; then we'd have to give high doses of insulin to get their blood sugar down. Here again, Dr. Hamilton advised me on treatment.

There was no drug specific for sepsis at that time. One day Dr. McNabb told me he had read in the medical journal about giving mercurochrome in the vein to treat sepsis. Now mercurochrome is a mercury derivative and highly poisonous, yet he had me go ahead and give some to one fellow intravenously. But while we were still treating this man, Doris Kirkman, my girlfriend at that time, was coming down to Memphis, and I decided I needed off for a day or two. I got Dr. Stevens, still a student and a few quarters behind me, to cover for me. Then I asked Dr. McElroy for permission to get off. He did not directly refuse me, but asked, "What are you here for?" "I'm here to see if I can learn something," I said. "Well, maybe it'd be better if you stayed." But I took off anyway.[1]

When I came back on the ward after the weekend, a number of new patients had come in. Some, of course, had been there before I left and I was familiar with their cases—a typhoid case and some pneumonia cases.

Well, McElroy heard that I had been off, so he decided to pour the heat on me for that. On the Thursday after my weekend off, he had all 20-plus interns and residents of the hospital meet on my ward to accompany him and me on our rounds.

Dr. McElroy led and I followed, with the others behind me as we went from bed to bed. Of course, I could tell him about the patients I was familiar with. When we came to new patients, I'd look down on their charts to read the diagnosis, and would try to tell him about a case I had previously dealt with that had the same diagnosis. For one new case, I looked on the chart and saw "bleeding ulcer," so I said that was his diagnosis. "Did you see him bleed?" "No, sir," I said, "I took his word for it." "Well, if he told you he did, you could go mighty quick up there to the bathroom and see if he bled." "Well, yes, sir; I didn't do it." "Well, how do you treat ulcers?" I mentioned using Sippy Powders. "What's in Sippy Powders; do you know?" I didn't know how much sodium carbonate, calcium carbonate, was in it. "Well, you see how dumb you are? You'll *never* make a doctor!"

Unfortunately, we came to the patient with sepsis and I told McElroy about giving him mercurochrome intravenously. "What did you say you gave that fellow? Mercurochrome. Dr. McNabb said we'd try it; he'd read about it...." "Mercurochrome? In the vein? I wouldn't give it to my dog! Don't you know what mercurochrome will do—mercury? It'll destroy the kidneys; he may have hemorrhage of the bowels!"— and I don't know what all he said—"Listen, man, you're not *about* to make a doctor! You don't know *anything!* You're so dumb it's pitiful!" And I heard some of the interns behind me murmuring, "Uh-oh! He's blowing off now like he used to years ago."

And for one hour, all through my ward round, Dr. McElroy did his best to humiliate me, chastising me for taking off.

I saw one patient brought into the medical ward with part of his head cut off, from the bridge of his nose to the crown of his head. Another fellow had chopped him with an axe; you could look down through his head and out his nose. The front of his cerebrum—the seat of reason—was gone. But we put *dura*[2] over his brain, and he lived. If given food, he would eat, but he had no reason. I've always wondered what happened to him.

One night a fellow was sent to me with locked bowels; he was having colic. I did a rectal exam and hit something firm. I thought maybe he had swallowed a bone, perhaps the shoulder blade of a rabbit. But after giving a spinal injection to relax him, I got him in bed and had the nurse get me gauze and a forceps. I went up in his rectum to look, and pulled out a few persimmon seeds. I said, "Well, my goodness alive!" I gave him enemas, and broke up the mass with an instrument. Finally the material began to come out—nearly a panful of persimmon seeds! Later I asked the fellow, "Mister, how in the world could you go under a persimmon tree and eat that many persimmons and swallow that many seeds?" And I told him, "You might not believe this, but this is what came out of your rectum."

Other rotations

From Medicine, I went to Pediatrics for one month, then to OB for two months. I guess I delivered 125 to 150 babies, because we had deliveries just about every day, and sometimes two in labor at the same time.

I happened to go on my Isolation rotation during the meningitis epidemic. The isolation ward was in a separate facility; soon all patients entering the hospital who complained of a headache were being sent down to Isolation until we proved that they didn't have meningitis. We'd have to do a spinal puncture and run the spinal fluid in the lab while watching the patient for a day or two to rule out this disease. We even saw cases of "meningiphobia" (excessive fear of meningitis), and we isolated cases of strep throat, encephalitis, tuberculosis, chicken pox, measles, mumps, and scarlet fever, along with the meningitis cases. Usually we would send the measles and mumps cases back home to recover.

I did so many spinal punctures while in Isolation that I finally said, "I don't care if I never do another one." (Later in life, however, I gave a lot of spinal anesthetics for Dr. Clemmer in Milan.) The resident physician over me was Dr. "Shorty" Dees, who later went to Jackson, Mississippi, and became a surgeon. He wrote an article, published in a medical journal, on putting powdered sulphur in the abdomen to treat a ruptured appendix.

My final rotation was in gynecology, or GYN. Dr. Williams was the head of the Department of Gynecology. We dealt with just about any conceivable type of problem: tumors, abdominal pregnancies, and so forth. Once we thought we were taking out a tumor, but when we removed the mass, it was a fetus that had already calcified—an abdominal pregnancy that went four or five months before the fetus died. We had cases of multilocular cyst, adenoma, cancer, and ovarian cysts. One patient's tumor was as large as a pumpkin; we had to cut her abdomen both vertically and laterally to get it out.

One day I was in GYN with Dr. Hugh Dent Johnson, who later went to Montgomery, Alabama, as a surgeon. He did a hysterectomy where the womb had fibrosed with the bowels. "Dr. Johnson," I said, "I believe you took out part of the bowel with that mass. Put a colon tube up in her rectum and see how far it goes." So he stuck this colon tube in her rectum and it hit a dead end. "Oh, goodness!" he said, and it really hurt him. So we tried to bring the bowel down from above and connect it to the rectal colon. I don't remember whether the patient lived or died. Soon after that I got off GYN.

Venereal diseases

We had a case of syphilis of the central nervous system (CNS). I can visualize that man now, over on the left side of the ward, about halfway down. We were having to catheterize him, and a nurse accompanied me as I did the procedure. First we washed the area with sterile water, then we cleaned it with a very dilute phenol (carbolic acid) solution. The nurse handed me what I thought was this solution, and I swabbed the head of the man's penis with it. Then I noticed the skin starting to turn white and asked, "Honey, what was that you gave me?" She looked and said, "Lord, Doctor, that's full-strength phenol!" "Give me that alcohol, quick!" I slapped the alcohol on his penis, but the acid had burned the patient so that the opening of the penis, called the meatus, was constricted. We inserted a catheter to maintain an opening. But every time I'd go around that ward till he died, that man would point down between his legs and say, "Doctor, doctor! What you gonna do for this?"

I felt bad about what had happened, and this mistake really hurt the nurse. I said, "Honey, that'll teach us to be sure and look at the bottle to know what we're doing from now on." The man finally died of advanced- phase syphilis.

All this was going on during the construction of the new John Gaston Hospital, and we saw ambulatory patients in a temporary barracks. Syphilis was quite common then. Primary syphilis could be cured if caught in time. Secondary syphilis might invade some parts of the body and leave permanent damage. Tertiary, or advanced-phase syphilis, was a massive invasion of the organs, and fatal. So, before penicillin came and gave us a simple and effective treatment for syphilis, I was able to see the disease in all its stages.

Some patients with advanced syphilis had aortic aneurysms; their aorta (the large vessel coming off the top of the heart that branches into arteries) would balloon out. On one patient, the aneurism got so big it just eroded the chest until he had a mass as big as a coconut protruding out. When you put your hand on it, you could feel the blood pulsing. It finally ruptured and killed the patient, a young black man.

Our treatment for syphilis in the 1930s was to give Salversan, a yellow liquid containing heavy bismuth, by injection or intravenously. We interns would go out to Eve Hall and have a clinic twice a week in the evening, and golly bill! It was like a camp meeting—200 or 300 syphilis patients.

Rod Stewart was rooming and interning with me. So we'd go over to give shots together. We would just move around among the patients; the nurse would fill the syringe and I would stick them; we'd do three or four patients at the same time. Stewart would say, "Hey now! If you want to be treated good, if you want me to treat you nice, come put a half-dollar in this hat!" He'd get a hatful of half-dollars, and durned if I could get a penny!

Stewart would bring his hat back to our room and I'd say, "Golly, Stewart, how many did you get today?" He'd say, "Looka here." I'd say, "I couldn't get a one out of 'em." He'd laugh about it, and would always say, "Now, I'm gonna make money!"

For treating gonorrhea, or 'clap,' we had a stand supporting a container filled with a solution. With this solution, we would irrigate the patient, forcing the liquid into his bladder, then drain it out again, in an attempt to fight infection and to drain the pus. Years later we realized that what we were *really* doing was forcing the pus back into his bladder, possibly infecting his epididymis and testicles. Without treatment, the inflammation would cause a stricture of the urethra. We would have done better to let the infection localize.

(When I came to Medina, Dr. Thompson at Jackson was a genitourinary (GU) man, and was still using the method we employed at John Gaston. The patient would develop a stricture, and for the rest of his life would have to come back periodically for dilation so he could urinate.)

New drugs

When penicillin came, we thought, *Oh, we've got something for syphilis now!* We would give a shot or two of that, and the problem would be solved. When penicillin first came out, it cost six or seven dollars a shot, and we thought that was awful. But it nearly wiped out gonorrhea and syphilis.

I saw other diseases as an intern that later were to be totally—or nearly —eradicated by new drugs. For instance, I saw lobar pneumonia; you'd listen to the chest, and it would sound completely solid, with no elasticity. After new drugs were available, it might take some time to get a response, and you'd still hear the solid sound, but the patient's temperature would drop to normal and we'd say, "Golly, isn't that something!" The pneumonia would be arrested, but it would take time for lysis (liquefaction) to take place and for the body to absorb the buildup in the lungs.

I've heard old Dr. Herron Sanford at Jackson say, "Whoopee! whoopee! We've got a drug now; we won't even have to operate for appendicitis!" Of course, this proved not to be true.

Romance

While I was interning, Lillie May Leake[3] was attending the U.T. School of Nursing and training in Memphis General Hospital. I met her on the OB ward and began to get interested. Then when I was at the isolation hospital, I'd watch through the window as she walked back to the nurses' living quarters. I'd see her wearing that little blue-gray uniform with pinstripes, a white collar, white cuffs and apron

and a white cap, and carrying scissors in her hand. I'd say, "That's the sweetest-looking girl that I nearly ever saw, and she's always so pleasant and kind!"

Left: Lillie May Leake when she graduated from U.T. School of Nursing in 1935, at age 24. *Right:* Dr. Robert Morris, intern, and Lillie Leake, student nurse, during their engagement. Both were in training at Memphis General Hospital (later renamed John Gaston Hospital), and both completed their training on Dec. 31, 1935; they were married later that same day. Stamped on reverse, with blanks filled in by hand: "Made by Avery Co./July 17, 1934 /... / Memphis, Tenn."

Lillie May says that I was such a hungry-looking fellow, so tired from working night and day, that she felt sorry for me. Sometimes we couldn't even get time off to eat; so she would bring me a little bit of food. The other fellows noticed Lillie May, too, and someone would ask, "Who's she going with?" And they'd say, "That Morris boy yonder. I don't know what she sees in *him!*" But it was true that the hospital staff really liked her; she had a pleasant manner, was good at her work, and was cooperative. This was true in the operating room, on the ward, wherever she'd go.

So I often got to see my sweetie while I was on the ward. We'd talk, and got closer and closer. She finished her nurse's training the very day I finished my internship—December 31st, 1935. I received the last internship diploma from Memphis General Hospital, as well as the first key to John Gaston Hospital, because Memphis General was being renamed John Gaston and was opening the next day for full service.

Lillie May's uncle, Farrer Leake,[4] was superintendent over building the forms for John Gaston Hospital. When I think now of those huge concrete piers, with so much iron in them, and what a nice hospital it was, it seems a shame that they're now tearing it down to build a new one.[5]

CHAPTER X

MARRIAGE, AND PRACTICE IN GIBSON

Wedding and honeymoon

Only a few hours after Lillie May and I received our diplomas—hers in nursing and mine for rotating internship— we were married. Papa and my brother John had come down, bringing Bro. J. L. Robertson, our pastor, whom I had asked to perform the ceremony. Following the graduation exercises, we drove to the Leake home at Greenlevel, four miles north of Collierville. Here Lillie May's family had prepared for our wedding, which took place late in the afternoon. My brother John was best man, and the bridesmaid was Winifred Dobbins, Lillie's cousin. Unfortunately, Brother Robertson had piles (painful hemorrhoids), so before our wedding I gave him two belladonna and opium suppositories. But their effect was the opposite of what I had hoped for: He turned pale, became nauseated, and barely made it through the ceremony. Still, we were lawfully and happily wed.

John drove Papa, Bro. Robertson, Lillie May, and myself back to Gibson that very night, so we newlyweds could spend our honeymoon in my grandfather's home. There, we went upstairs to the north room and, as they say, consummated our marriage.

Starting in practice

You would think that, after finishing many months of training, and following an exhausting day in which we graduated and were married—especially considering that it was New Year's Eve—we would be entitled to a leisurely honeymoon. However, the very next morning, January 1st, 1936, Grover Bratcher came to the house wanting me to see him about a backache. Dr. Hunt, though still alive, was now 89 years old and had retired some years before. Since his retirement, the only doctor remaining in Gibson was Dr. Rozzell. Throughout my medical training, everyone at home assumed that I would return to Gibson and practice medicine there. So that is what I began to do.

Dr. Morris and daughter Una (Morris) Grant in front of house where both were born (see Chapter 2 for other photos). The newly-wed Morrises moved into this house in January 1936, and Una was born October 31 that same year. Photo taken in early to mid-1980s; the house has since burned down.

Papa and Mama had moved in with Dr. Hunt to care for him, and this left their former home, my birthplace, vacant; so Lillie May and I moved into that house. One room we arranged as an office; the dining room became a treatment room, and the parlor served as a reception area. Our living quarters were in the other side of the house. I borrowed $600–$700 from Dr. Hunt to get started, spending some $400 on a second-hand Ford and the rest on medical equipment, supplies, and other furnishings for the office.

Medical practice, of course, was not the same then as now: We didn't have all the many different drugs for specific diseases, and I could carry most of my medicines in one bag. Back then, in the late 1930s, we were using Atebrin and quinine for malaria, Anatoxin for meningitis, and a few other drugs. Sometimes we treated meningitis without drugs, simply by draining the spinal fluid to relieve the pressure. With that alone, patients quite often survived. Sulfa drugs and penicillin did not become available until several years after I arrived in Medina, during World War II.

Not long after beginning to practice, I received a call from Dr. Rozzell. Cecil Chandler had come to see him, thinking he was dying. Dr. Rozzell told me, "Listen! I've got something over here, and I don't know what it is. I've given him one or two shots of morphine and I can't ease him." So I drove over to Dr. Rozzell's place; after examining Cecil, I asked him, "Have you been bitten by anything?" "Well, now, I *was* out there gathering corn, and something stung me on the leg. I slapped it through my breeches, but never did see it." "I'll bet you've been bitten by a black widow spider. I've seen a few cases down there in Memphis like this, your belly being as hard as it is and hurting you so."

So I went back to my house to get either calcium gluconate or calcium chloride, returned, and injected it in the patient's vein. Cecil said, "Oh, that sure has helped me!" I said, "Dr. Rozzell, this is arachnoidism, from the black widow spider." He said, "I never heard of it!" and I replied, "Well, I never did either, till I was down there and happened to see a case."

Dr. Hunt's death

Dr. Hunt was very happy to see me back home and practicing medicine. Besides the money he loaned me to buy a car and medical equipment, he had helped me through medical school, paying for my room ($35 a month), my tuition ($195 or $200 a quarter), and my books. We thought it was something awful, back then, to pay $25 for an anatomy book. My daddy had helped me with minor expenses, such as clothes and pocket money, but my grandfather had paid the major expenses.

I had not been practicing in Gibson many months when Grandpa Hunt got strep throat. He developed a high fever and became delirious; we found him walking around in the yard. His throat became so inflamed and his neck so swollen that he labored to breathe. I had Dr.

Berryhill come from Jackson to see him; Berryhill recommended that he be hospitalized.

Grandpa didn't want to go to the hospital, but I kept insisting until he finally gave in: "Robert, I'm 90 years old and my time has come. But if nothing else will satisfy you, I will go." And as we went out the door of his home, he spoke words that I clearly remember: "Robert, there's no need of me going to the hospital. I've been looking for this a long time. The Lord will do *exactly* what He said He'd do; so let's go!"

Dr. Hunt in his eighties, around 1930, when he had only a mustache. He paid the cost of tuition and books for his grandson and namesake, Robert Hunt Morris, to attend medical school, then died the year that the latter began practicing medicine (1936).

I carried Grandpa to Ousler's Clinic in Humboldt. It happened that a well-known ear, nose, and throat specialist from Memphis, named Dr. Shea, had come to Humboldt to see Mr. Bryant of Milan, and I was able to get him to look at Grandpa. The next day, Dr. Shea gave Grandpa a mild anesthetic and lanced his throat to insert tubes. The swelling in his throat subsided, and we became hopeful of his recovery. Lillie May was staying there with him, nursing him, and I spent as much time with him as I could. Grandpa had been in the clinic several days when one day, following a visit with him, I left to answer a call from a patient in Gibson who had a pea or bean in his ear; I thought it wouldn't hurt to be gone that long. As I left, Dr. Hunt was talking to M. Hunt about things in the past. Grandpa's mind had always been very alert, and he had a remarkable memory for dates. Mr. M. said, "I think I'll go home for dinner"; so, as I was leaving too, only Lillie May was left with Dr. Hunt.

But when I got back to the clinic after seeing my patient, Lillie May told me, "He's dead." "He's *dead?* What happened?" "Well," she said, "he just turned, laid his head over on my bosom, and died." I said, "Well, if I'd known that, I wouldn't have left. I'm sort of surprised." But I had the satisfaction of hearing him say that the Lord would do exactly what He said He'd do. Dr. Hunt died as Grandpa Morris had done, confident in the Lord.

CHAPTER XI
DECISION TO MOVE

I have always considered Dr. Rozzell a fine man and a friend as well as a Christian. But after I had been in Gibson a while, some of his former patients chose to come to me, and when Dr. Rozzell found this out, he was reported to have said, "I don't see why you'd see *him*, when I've been taking care of you all these years." While I understood this feeling, of course I could not refuse to treat whoever came to me. I began seriously considering a move and discussing it with Lillie May. Finally we reached a decision to move away from Gibson.

So, following Dr. Hunt's death, I began actively searching for other possible locations to practice medicine. I had gone out to visit Steele, Missouri, during my internship; now I seriously considered Bolivar, Tennessee. I knew Dr. Dorris, a general surgeon in Memphis, whose father practiced in Bolivar and was wanting to retire. Dr. Dorris suggested I rent his father's office and take over his practice, but he added one condition: that I send him my general surgery patients. I said, "Doctor, I'm not going to tie myself up with any doctor, promising that I will send him my patients. Now I would say this: If your patient came to me and said he wanted you, I would send him to you. But I am going to keep the liberty of sending my patients to the doctor I want to refer them to." "Well," he said, "if that's it, I won't let you have it." So I turned Bolivar down.

I drove down to Lexington, Tennessee, and looked at the possibility of practicing there. Cornelia Huntsman, who had been in my class at medical school, was a general practitioner there and had office space to lease; her father had practiced there before her. But there were two other doctors in the town, and I didn't feel clear about such a move.

Meanwhile, Henry Hester was the pharmacist in Medina.[1] We were friends, having roomed together in Mrs. Ash's home in Memphis while I was studying medicine and he, pharmacy. During school vacations, we used to go courting together in Medina. We were seeing Cora Sims, Katherine Fly, Katherine Gowan, and a Pickins girl there. I had never been particularly attracted to the town, however; in fact, I believe I would have cried if someone had told me back then that I would be living in Medina one day.

But Henry now kept calling me: "This is a good field for practice; you ought to come over here." There had been three doctors in Medina, but Dr. Keaton had died, and shortly before this Dr. Hendrix had moved back to his home state of Alabama, leaving only Dr. Weldon Oliver, who was getting along in years.

Finally one day I spoke my feelings out loud to my dad, telling him what Dr. Rozzell was reported to be saying. "Well," I said, "I'll tell you what I'm going to do. I'm going to get out from under that. I'll just go over to Medina and practice, and I won't be hearing such things." Hearing me say this nearly killed my family. My mother, especially, tried to talk us out of moving from our home next door to hers. But by this time, we had made up our minds. So in April 1937 we moved, following Una's birth in Gibson on October 31 the previous year. (Dr. Rozzell, by the way, attended her birth.)

Looking back, I believe the Lord impressed me to go to Medina, although the reasons given above were instrumental. Henry Hester's asking me to come and Dr. Rozzell's attitude were things God used to bring about our move. So I reckon I've been where I was supposed to be. And yet I've worked my tail off in Medina; I've gotten up many a night to see patients.

A tribute to Dr. Weldon Oliver[2]

When I came to Medina, I opened an office upstairs over the bank. Dr. Oliver was in the front part; I was up another flight and in the back. I stayed there till 1950. Dr. Oliver was one of the most unselfish men I ever knew. He never made me feel like we were competing with each other. Patients had to walk up the steps and right by his door in order to reach my office. Having our offices in the same building and our homes just across the street from one another brought Dr. Oliver and me into contact with each other almost every day; we would speak, shake hands, and literally rub shoulders passing in the stairway. We would ride together to our county medical meetings, which were held monthly in Trenton at that time, and when it was cold we would lay his buggy lap spread across our knees. My water for ordinary home uses came from a cistern, but I would go over to Dr. Oliver's house every day for drinking water. Frequently I ate special foods in his home, and sometimes regular meals, since Miss Maggie Cole, the sister of his deceased wife, was living with him and his sons and keeping house for them. Since we were in such close contact, I can speak with first-hand knowledge of Dr. Oliver's character.

From the beginning of our friendship until his death, Weldon Oliver manifested good morals, unselfishness, and dependability. He showed kindness and patience in his home; he loved visitors, was friendly to neighbors, and was good to his patients. He was a tolerant man, a stable citizen, and loyal to his church. I can see him now, chuckling and laughing, his whole body shaking, and spitting between two fingers held to his lips.

Many times Dr. Oliver called me into his office to see a patient and to give my opinion as to diagnosis and treatment. Seemingly it never crossed his mind that he might be losing a patient to me. Was this not unselfishness?

I recall carrying Dr. Oliver to see his brothers in Columbia, Tennessee, one year on Mule Day. His brothers were in auto sales and service there. It was pleasant riding together and conversing on the way, and I enjoyed meeting his relatives and seeing the town and the wonderful mules.

He attended the birth of our second daughter, Trebor, which we much appreciated.

Dr. Oliver had several angina attacks. I talked with him about these pains, what they meant, and what could happen. One day he complained of his arms aching severely and said, "I feel like my bones are going to burst." After taking his pulse and blood pressure (which had fallen), and noting his moist skin, I said, "Dr. Oliver, you have had a coronary artery occlusion. You must stay in bed for three weeks or more without exercising, and I will instruct you what to do later."

After about two weeks in bed, he seemed to be doing well. Then one evening I came home late but told Lillie May I would go over and see Dr. Oliver before eating supper. She went over with me, and we found his sons Wilbur and Dalton with him. I greeted him and asked how he felt. "As usual," was his reply. I took his pulse and blood pressure, and listened to his heart. "What is my blood pressure?" he asked. I told him; then, after laying my instruments down on the nearby chest of drawers, I pulled a chair up to the bed so we could talk.

Suddenly his body stiffened, his arm drew up, his head fell backward, then he relaxed again. "Boys," I said, "your father is dying." I injected adrenalin and worked with him a few minutes, then announced, "It's useless; he's dead."

One part of Medina not radically changed since Dr. Morris's early years there is the Medina Cotton Gin, still in operation. The gin is only ¼ mile from the current Morris home. This picture taken in late 1980s by RMII.

I can truthfully say that Dr. Weldon Oliver was a lovely man and a real friend.

Dr. Oliver's passing away left me as Medina's only physician, which remained the case throughout the rest of my career.

CHAPTER XII

SETTLING AND PRACTICING IN MEDINA

Lillie May and I, along with our five-month-old daughter, Una Deane, came to Medina in April 1937. Papa helped me move our personal belongings, as well as my medical equipment, in a horse-drawn wagon. We carried the equipment upstairs to my new office over the bank. Papa and I both cried all the way from Gibson to Medina. I hated to leave my parents, yet felt that I should.

House and home

We first rented a house built by Robert Senter that was owned by the Methodist parson. This house, at 325 East Church Street, still stands today. I told Bro. Childress, "Go ahead and fix it up, and I'll tell you what: I'll rent it long enough to pay for your fixing it." So he had it freshly painted and had the floors and the fireplace grates repaired. We bought a stove from Mr. Jim Bass for cooking—a small oil-burner. Lillie May canned on that with a pressure cooker. A cistern, encased in the back porch, collected rainwater that we used for cleaning and washing. The barrier around the cistern was inadequate, and as Una grew into a toddler, my mother worried so much about the possibility of her falling into it that she had trouble sleeping when visiting our home. Fortunately the nightmare never actually happened.

Without my knowing it, Bro. Childress arranged to sell the house that we were renting to Chester Fly. When I found this out, I said, "Bro. Childress, if you'd told me you wanted to sell this house, I might have bought it." And in fact, I did buy it from Chester Fly, borrowing the money to do so. We lived in this house a total of two years, during which time I had a two-car garage built.

In 1939, a man whose name I'll leave blank began asking me, "What about me trading my home for yours?" He had a larger house on Main Street, adjoining the schoolyard. At first I wasn't interested, since I had already gone into debt and was reluctant to borrow more money. But after some time had passed, and after asking me two or three times without getting a definite answer, he tried to pin me down: "Well, what will you do?" He wanted $2250 and my house in exchange for his house. Finally I said, "Yes, I will trade with you, but I'll have to go and see if I can get the money." People in Medina probably wondered where I would get it, but as my family members in Gibson were close friends of Nestor James, the banker there, I was able to get a loan from him, with my grandfather Dr. Hunt cosigning.[1] Well, when I told Mr.———that I had the money to trade, he surprised me by saying, "No, I won't do it for $2250. But I *will* do it for $2500."

Well, here was Lillie May with two babies (Trebor had been born on July 4, 1938) and with our goods already packed up in boxes, ready to move. In fact, we were going to share a truck with the ———s, first moving our goods to their former home, then moving theirs to ours. Lillie May had been waiting that Monday morning for me to come with the truck, but now the morning had passed and I was facing the demand for another $250 which I didn't have. I said, "Mr. ———, I wouldn't have thought you'd have done that-a-way; I thought you'd do what you said you'd do. But I'm going to move you *today*." I got a truck and started hauling our goods to the house on Main Street, and went and got the extra $250 in Gibson. And now we've been here 50 years.

The first Morris home in Medina, at 325 Church Street, built by Robert Senter. The Morrises first rented, then purchased, this house, adding a two-car garage. They lived here from 1937 to 1939; Trebor (Morris) Ambrose was born here on July 4, 1938. Photo by LLM, 1987.

We hadn't been living here long when my sister Evelyn came over one day and stepped through the floor in the northeast corner of the living room. So the floor was rotting in that corner! Later we found out that the ———s had believed that termites were in the flooring, but that proved not to be true. The builder had not finished the trim around the front windows properly; the window sill was merely flush with the bricks rather than overhanging them. The mortar covering the joint allowed water to seep in between the sill and the bricks, and to run down between the floor and subfloor, rotting them out.

Relatives help Dr. and Mrs. Morris celebrate their daughter Una's first birthday in October 1937. Adults are *(from left):* Sy Mincey, Evelyn (Morris) Mincey (Evelyn is Robert's sister), Joe Morris (his father), Robert Morris himself, Bernice Morris (his mother), and Lillie Morris. Una toddles away while cousin Bobby Joe Mincey, sitting on the grass, watches.

The Morris "House by the Road" (reference is to a familiar poem: "Let me live in a house by the side of the road, and be a friend to man"), at 310 North Main Street, Medina. In 1939, Dr. Morris traded his house on Church Street, plus $2500 cash, for this larger one, where he remained the rest of his life. Photo by LLM, 1985.

So I got Mr. Will Turner and Mark Williford to make repairs. I said, "Mark, y'all tear this floor out. Open the two north windows and pitch the wood outside; then put another floor in." I don't remember whether any of the joists had to be replaced or not, but they made a good repair and put in a new white oak flooring. (Our wainscoting out in the hall is made from the flooring they pulled up.) Now, however, I had this additional expense to cope with.

The "Little House"

Later, when World War II began and Milan Arsenal was developed (we called it "the Arsenal" or "the Area"), and we had four children, we built a little two-room house out back as rental property. Lillie May also thought that, with her mama and papa getting older and all their boys being in the armed services, they might want to move up here from Germantown with their daughter Bess, who was still quite young. We did rent out the "Little House" for a while. But after the war, with three more children (Brenda Leake was born May 20, 1940; Robert Hunt, December 5. 1941; and Lillie Katherine, November 11, 1944), our main house began to get crowded, and Lillie May and I considered the best way to increase our living space. I had a contractor figure the cost of building new rooms on our existing house, and he estimated $3500 for the job, a sizable sum back then. But Lillie May was convinced that we could move the Little House and join it to our big house cheaper;[2] also, we were tired of having renters. Unfortunately, when the Little House was moved, it was set on brick pillars rather than on a solid foundation, and it eventually settled in places.

The "Little House," after being attached to the rear of the brick house. Photo taken around 1950, before siding was added.

After the Little House had been rolled up to the main house, and while the two buildings were still being joined, I came home one day to find Mr. Gately on the roof with a sledgehammer, knocking off my slate shingles. I had intended for him to dovetail the slate in with the roof of the Little House, but he had decided to bring one roof under the other. I said, "Mr. Gately, *what* are you doing? Don't break my shingles! Don't ruin my roof! Quit now! I'll get someone else." Then I got Ira Bell and Penick McLemore—and I think Fred Irby—to work on it. But they had to bring the roof of the Little House in a little below the other roof. Before all this was over, we spent more to move the Little House than we would have spent to build new rooms. I've regretted that decision ever since.

My mother's death

My mother, Bernice Hunt Morris, called "Mama Bee" in her last years, died in 1939. I had been in Medina a little under two years, and she had come over to see our second child, Trebor, who was just learning to walk. Then one day I made a call to Gibson to see Emma Estes, the wife of Rick Estes, a former Gibson County sheriff. As I drove past the home place, Mama was coming across the lawn toward the gate carrying a dressed chicken. I stopped to say hello, and asked, "Where are you going with that chicken?" She said, "I'm going over to Liz Kiser's to give it to her." I told her where I was going, we chatted a minute or so, then I drove off.

After seeing Mrs. Estes, I returned to Medina, and less than an hour later got a call from Papa saying, "Come over and see your mother; she's sick." "I said, "What in the world has happened? I just talked to her at the gate when I was making that call!" He said, "I don't know. She's out here deathly sick; she's vomiting and suffering bad." So I turned around and drove right back to Gibson. Mama was out on the back steps, red in the face, vomiting, and complaining of her stomach. We got her in bed, and I told Papa, "I'm not sure, but it may be acute gall bladder. She's vomiting and is sore in her abdomen." I gave Mama a medication to ease her, and had Dr. Clemmer come over from Milan (the next day, I believe). He, too, diagnosed her as having gall bladder trouble. But looking back today, I wonder instead whether Mama's indigestion really indicated a heart attack.

After several days had gone by, perhaps a week, I could see that Mama was dying. Her blood pressure fell and her pulse was rapid. I knew my father was sitting up with her at night, and I kept running back and forth between Medina and Gibson. One morning, after sitting up all night, Papa said, "Robert, last night Mother told me, 'Joe, you've been as true as gold to me all my life.' I wouldn't take a pretty for that, Son, I never knew any woman —never *touched* any woman— until I married your mama." I said, "Well, that is wonderful."[3]

Mama died the very day after this conversation. Her death was as difficult as any I've seen. She struggled for breath, and even though I gave her one or two shots to ease her, she fought for breath till she died.

Practice in and around Medina

I practiced medicine in Gibson County and in four of the surrounding counties—Crockett, Madison, Henderson, and Carroll (occasionally Weakley too), usually working within a 20-mile radius of my home. I made house calls and maintained an office for medicine and minor surgery. I also related to several hospitals, but primarily, until late in my practice, Milan Hospital and St. Mary's Hospital, since they were closest. Milan Hospital, in Milan, was owned by Dr. Hubert P. Clemmer, and originally called Clemmer's Clinic; it was built in a

T-shape by Dr. Clemmer's father. St. Mary's, in Humboldt, was run by a Catholic order.

I sent most of my obstetrical patients to Milan Hospital, as well as patients requiring general surgery—common surgery such as appendix and gall bladder removals. Usually Clemmer would operate and I'd assist. Later I gave a lot of anesthetics for him, often using the anesthetic machine; and, as mentioned earlier, I gave a lot of spinal anesthetics. Some of my OB patients went to St. Mary's.

Robert and Lillie Morris with daughters Una *(foreground)*, Trebor *(with mother)*, and Brenda *(in father's arms)*. Reverse of photo gives this information: Taken May 23, 1940, when Brenda was three days old, by Merrel McAdoo, assisted by Joel Bradbury. Enlargement of original was a gift to parents from Trebor (Morris) Ambrose, November 1977.

Over the years, I worked increasingly with doctors and hospitals in the larger city of Jackson, a few miles farther from Medina. As in Humboldt and Milan, I delivered babies, administered anesthetics, and assisted in surgery. I sent many patients to Drs. McClearin, Batten, and Pierce at the old Memorial Hospital, as well as to Dr. Webb at his small hospital, and, after it opened, to colleagues at the Doctors' Hospital. Then, when the larger, better- equipped Jackson-Madison County General Hospital was completed, I became a staff physician there,[4] working with Chandler, Riddler, Hubbard, and George Dodson. I sent many OB and surgery patients there in my later years.

Throughout my career, I sent some of my more difficult cases to Memphis. For surgery, I referred patients most often to Tom West, occasionally to R. L. Sanders, and once or twice to Chrisler. For neurosurgery, I made referrals to Dr. Eustis Sims and Dr. O'Neal. I sent a few unusual orthopedic cases to Dr. Speed and Dr. Francis Mitchell at Campbell's Clinic.

Two early prescriptions written by Dr. Morris. See footnote no. 1 in chapter 11 for Williams Drug Store.

Obstetrics

I did a lot of deliveries—a career total of some 2500 babies— both in hospitals and in homes.[5] Having patients in different hospitals kept me trotting back and forth from one to the other, and sometimes caused conflicts in my schedule. I would have preferred to centralize my obstetrics in Milan, but some patients felt strongly about going to Humboldt or Jackson instead. Many a time I'd be delivering a baby in one hospital, for instance Milan, when Lillie May would phone saying, "You've got another patient ready for delivery, over in Humboldt."

Once I was delivering in Jackson when Milan Hospital phoned, saying, "You've got a patient over here that will soon be ready to deliver." "Well, I'm not through with the delivery *here* yet," I said. A little later they called again: "Dr. Morris, are you coming?" "Yes, just as quick as I get through." Well, I finished up and was rushing to Milan when I got caught behind a procession with President Truman in it, going to Trenton. There was nothing I could do but stay in that line, all the way to Milan. And when I finally got to the hospital there, the patient had already given birth; the nurses had had to get either Dr. Clemmer or Dr. Fields to attend her. The father met me at the door and said, "You're just too damned late!" "Well, I'm sorry," I said. "I left just as quick as I could, but I got caught in this line here with the President." But that didn't satisfy him.

In another incident, Dr. Fields had tended a patient for me that had gone into precipitate labor. He had just gone in to examine the mother and baby, tie the cord, and see that everything was all right. When I talked to him about it, he said, "You just go ahead and collect the insurance"—it wasn't but $25—"and you can take care of a patient for me sometime." So I filled out the insurance forms, and Dr. Fields gave the fee to me. But the patient and her husband were upset with me for getting that money, and although I tried to explain how Dr. Fields had told me to keep the fee that otherwise would have gone to him, they never forgave me for that.

House calls

Principally, my practice was small-town and rural. I made house calls in Milan, Humboldt, Jackson, and Oakfield, on Christmasville Road, and out to Lavinia, Spring Creek, Law, Blue Goose, and places like that. I was on the trot constantly, which made it hard to keep consistent office hours. When I'd come back to my office after a call, someone would say, "I've been waiting for you for an hour or two." I'd say, "Well, I've been to Oakfield"—or perhaps Law—"and got into something and couldn't get away." Still, I did have regular office hours posted: 8:30–11:30 a.m. and 1:30–4:30 p.m. I kept to them the best I could, but usually stayed till 5:30 or 6:00 p.m., and then often had to go back after supper.

Many a time I was called to a home in the middle of the night. Often it would be to deliver a baby, because the patient had refused my advice to go to a hospital. Expense was a big factor, of course. Then too, they'd say, "Mama has had five (or six) children at home, and I'm not about to go to a hospital. If you can't deliver it, I'll get somebody else." So until the 1960s, I did a lot of deliveries in the home. I had a steel case for my obstetrical instruments, a gift from Dr. Ben Penn in

Humboldt. Among my instruments were some I had been given by Dr. Waller in Spring Creek. To sterilize the instruments, Lillie May would boil them in this steel case on our stove; she would also sterilize linens in her pressure cooker. So I carried this case of instruments, as well as my two regular leather bags, when I did home deliveries.[6]

One night I was called to Law to see a new patient. Harvey Pillar said, "You see that light 'way over yonder?" "Yeah, I see it, but I'm not going to carry all these bags to that light. You'll have to help me carry 'em." So I carried one while he carried the other two; then when he got tired, we switched. But I did a lot of that kind of stuff.

A familiar sight in the Morris home for more than 50 years: a leather doctor's bag by the front door.

Dr. Waller

The physician in Spring Creek when I first came to Medina, was Dr. Elmer E. Waller. When he became unable to practice medicine, I treated him, and many of his former patients began calling me. Also, Waller was the brother-in-law of the school principal at Three Way, Mr. Fesmire, who was greatly admired in the community as a good administrator and disciplinarian. Since I was treating Dr. Waller, Mr. Fesmire began coming to see me with his wife, and they thought the world of me, which caused my practice to grow in the Three Way community, When Mrs. Fesmire became critically ill, I sent her to Leland Johnson in Jackson; he increased her medication, and we continued treating her till she died.

Ambulance service

Ambulance service, when needed, was provided by Menton Replogle, who owned the Medina Funeral Home. Menton and I were friends and, for a while, neighbors, but once I had to straighten out a knot in our relationship.

Early one morning I phoned Dr. Batten at Memorial Hospital in Jackson about a surgery case I was sending in. However, later in the day Batten phoned me back asking, "Bob, where is your patient?" I said, "I don't know. I told the ambulance where to take her—unless she backed out and wouldn't go. So I'll investigate and call you back."

I phoned the patient's home and asked where she was. "We had her taken to Dr. Webb's hospital." "Who told you to carry her there?" "Well, Menton told us, if it was him, he would take her to Dr. Webb." "Well, I thank you," I said. "I'll see him about it." So I phoned Dr. Batten, "Don't be looking for the patient. This undertaker has carried her to Dr. Webb's hospital, because they're big buddies. I'll deal with him, and I'm sorry it happened."

Opening day of Dr. Morris's medical office on Church Street, Medina, in September 1950— important to his practice but not mentioned in the text. Here Dr. and Mrs. Paul Wylie and children may be seen, as well as Una Deane, Lillie Katherine, Dr. Morris, and Robert Hunt (II). Building was designed by LLM. For a number of years Dr. Morris employed a receptionist, Ollie Herron, who was black. After the office was closed in 1970, it was rented out briefly as a dwelling, then sold to Johnny Leake, a nephew of LLM and an architect. He remodeled it extensively and later sold it. Directly behind this property is the First Baptist Church.

So one day I called Menton up to the office. "Menton," I said, "I want to tell you something, and you will hear it straight from me; you won't be hearing it down on the street. Why did you go out there and advise my patient to go to Dr. Webb's, when I had done made an appointment with another doctor at another hospital?" "Well," he said, "I thought it was better, and they wanted to go." I said, "They said you asked 'em and persuaded 'em to go there. But I want to tell you this, Menton: *You* are an undertaker, and you're driving the ambulance. And all you are supposed to do is to carry the patient where I direct you to carry him. If you can't do that, let me know. But if I tell you to take my patient one place, don't you *ever, EVER,* send him or persuade him to go anywhere else. 'Cause the only job you've got is to carry the patient to the hospital, and if he dies you can go and pick him up. But from now on, when I order one to go to a certain hospital, you do it. Now that's not gonna happen anymore; it had *better* not!"

Menton apologized, and I never had this problem again. Over the years, I had a good relationship with him, and Menton called me to treat him for his ailments. Eventually Menton developed angina, complaining of pain under the shoulder, then he had a severe spell and went to the hospital in Humboldt, where he died.

Bad debts

Most of my medical career was before the days of employer- provided health insurance and Medicaid. I had to rely on my patients paying out of their own pockets. Quite a few of them couldn't, and some *wouldn't,* pay all they owed. Some, I saw, were good, honest men, just poor. They would come and say, "Dr. Morris, I want to pay something on my bill. I know I owe you more, but I can't pay it all." Others, however, might say they couldn't pay me then, but would promise everything in the world. Then, as time went by, I would see them buying and doing things that cost good money, and I would think, *That fellow told me he didn't have any money a- tall.*[7] *And as many times as I've been to his house and delivered babies—and he won't pay me a penny!*

A few times I did resort to a bill collector to recover bad debts, until, after a couple of unpleasant experiences, I decided not to do that again. At one point I thought, *Well, I'll put these bills out for collection, and let this man collect them for me.* I had grown up with this man, and I had always heard that he was a good collector. So I gave him some accounts, but failed to keep copies of them for myself; I was just hoping some money would come in on these old accounts.

Well, a month or two passed, and when I asked the man, he claimed he hadn't collected anything yet. And, not remembering exactly what accounts I had given him, I pursued one debt on my own, having the Arsenal to garnishee the salary of a man living in West Station on Chapel Hill Road. So the man pulled up in front of my house one day, saying, "What is this you're doing? You're garnisheeing me to pay a debt, and I've got a receipt that I paid it!" He showed me the receipt, proving his point. To myself I said, *Whoa, this is not going to work!;* and aloud I said, "Mr. ———, I'm sorry." He continued: "You gave it to the wrong man to collect in the first place." I said, "I didn't know it; I thought he was honest. But I've never gotten it."

In fact, I never did get anything from that collector, and since I didn't know exactly what accounts I had given him, I didn't know how many others he might have collected. I scolded myself: *How foolish! I took him to be honest, and now I haven't got a record, and I don't know how many maybe HAVE paid and I don't know it, and I don't know how to post my books. Well, that'll never happen again!* So I quit even sending notices, and just let those debts go; I never knew whether the accounts had been paid.

There was another case where I delivered a baby for a man's wife. He had called me to his home, and when I arrived, I found the baby's arm sticking out. I had the woman taken to the hospital, and there we put her under an anesthetic, got the arm back inside the womb, then turned the baby around so it could be delivered. But the father never finished paying me. Many years later I delivered babies for two of his daughters, and each said she would pay me—or rather, that she would see that her father paid me. Then a year or two later one of them had another baby, born in Jackson. So I asked the Clinic, "Did you ever get your money?" "Yeah, we garnisheed their daddy and he paid it." This same man had gotten down in my living room floor begging me, "If you'll just come this time...I know I owe you. But please help me!" And I had replied, "Well, all right, I'll go, but I'm tired of this." I don't know how many babies I delivered for him and his children, but he never paid up his bill.

A few other times I pursued old debts by garnishment. For example, I gave the anesthetic to a woman at the Jackson hospital while a lump was being removed from her neck, driving there to do so, then back to Medina. I told the cashier, "I know these people. You be sure and collect my fee; otherwise I'll never get it." The fee was 20 or 25 dollars. Lo and behold, I never got paid. But a year or two later the patient was working in the plant in Milan, so I phoned up there and made her pay her bill. Well, this woman swelled up about that, and I reckon is mad at me to this day. Run-ins like this with my patients grieved me, so I said, "Well, I'll just quit that. I won't be garnisheeing any more to collect accounts."

In later years I sent out some statements on past-due accounts, but a year or two after retiring I quit, and never tried to collect any more.

Satisfaction in practice

The biggest hurdle I cleared in life was returning to medical school and finishing. Another personal victory was obtaining the coveted internship at Memphis General Hospital. And I feel satisfied with the place I chose to practice.

In and around Medina, I feel like I helped some people who otherwise would not have received the care they needed, and some who lacked the means to pay. I knew plenty of men who, with the families they had and their small income, had difficulty paying me, and I never sent them statements; I wouldn't worry them about their bill. Many poor people were honest, and if they got a little they would come and say, "Doctor, I can't pay my whole bill, but I want to give you this."

Then, too, many patients were my good friends, hard-working people, and would do exactly what they said they'd do; if they ever got the money, they would pay me. It was on the basis of this type of people that I made my living.[8]

CHAPTER XIII

TRAVEL, AND WORLD WAR II

Trip to Washington, D.C.

By the summer of 1940 our third child, Brenda, had been born, and life was going smoothly enough for me to take a rare vacation. Mama had died the previous year, and my father was now living alone in Dr. Hunt's house, with Guy and Sue nearby. So I took Papa, and he and I drove through the Great Smokies of East Tennessee to Asheville, North Carolina, and up along the Blue Ridge Mountains of Virginia through the Shenandoah Valley. Here we were impressed with the apple orchards and with the palatial homes where animals grazed on the front lawns.

Continuing toward Washington, we realized we were passing the Quantico Marine Base and decided to stop for a visit. Here on the parade grounds we saw an officer, a U.S. citizen but a native, we learned, of South Africa, yelling commands to young recruits: "Fall! ———!¹ Fire!" They were scrambling up and dropping down, getting up and down. I asked the officer showing us around, "Did you graduate from West Point?" He said, "No, I graduated from the University of Illinois. But I couldn't find a job then, so I went into the Service. Then I became an officer."

I said, "I tell you, they go through *something* in training." He said, "This is mild. Wait till they go through Parris Island. If they survive that, they can *do* it. But do you want to see something? Come back down here tomorrow, and there will be a sunset parade. All the big shots from Washington will be out here—the Undersecretary of the Army, top Marine officers, Pentagon officials. The old Marines are going to put on a parade for these young recruits." So Papa and I went on into Washington to get a room, and the next afternoon we returned. The parade ground was blacktopped, the size of a football field. You should have seen those Marines going through drills, presenting arms. The band played while the officials watched from a wooden stand and the young recruits from behind a rope fence.

Neither Papa nor I had ever been to Washington before. We called on the Representative from our district, Jere Cooper, whose home was in Dyersburg. When we entered his outer office, there sat Miss Hope Hart, one of my high school teachers. As soon as she saw me she said, "Well Robert Morris! I haven't seen you in years!" I was just as pleased and surprised to see her as she was me, and said, "Well, it's the first time I was ever in Washington." She said, "I'll tell you what I'll do. I'll give you some tickets, and you and your daddy can go to the House of Representatives today, and tomorrow you can go to the Senate." So we did that, going to the House, then to the Pentagon and the State building.

Jere Cooper happened to be serving as speaker *pro tem* in the House the day we visited. We were able to observe him conducting Congressional business, and thought he did it skillfully.

The next day, after visiting the Senate, we went to the Supreme Court building, where we saw the Justices' chambers and the courtroom. The Court was in its summer recess, however, so we didn't see any of the Justices themselves.

After this we visited the Bureau of Engraving, where we saw paper money being stamped out at an incredible rate. It seemed to us that every person in this department was black. As sheets of bills came off the press, the workers would feel them and cull any that didn't have the right feel.

We spent some time at the Smithsonian Institute, and the first thing we saw was all the dresses that Presidents' wives had worn to their inaugural balls. The next thing I recall is that we looked up, and there, suspended above us, was the *Spirit of St. Louis*, the plane Lindbergh had flown across the Atlantic. Then there were carriages and other forms of transportation, coins from around the world, rubber products, and communication devices. Finally I said, "I've seen so many things my head hurts!" I realized that the Smithsonian preserves a record of our progress in technology.

We had no card to visit the Department of State, but decided to step in there anyway. When we entered the State building, the guards didn't stop us, so we proceeded down a hall until I said, "Papa, there's Cordell Hull!" He was sitting in his office with his feet on the desk, reading. We didn't disturb him, and not seeing a guard, weren't sure how far we could go. But we got uneasy and didn't want to be ordered out, so we retreated.

We paid a brief visit to the Washington Cathedral, where we observed parts under construction as well as finished parts. The remains of some former Presidents, including Woodrow Wilson, lay under stone slabs along the wall. The massive stone columns, arches, and carvings were impressive to Papa and myself; neither of us had ever been in a cathedral.

Finally we had absorbed as much of Washington as we could take in, and our time was getting short, but being so close to New York City, I wondered if we couldn't squeeze in a quick side trip. "Papa," I asked, "what about us going to New York?" His instantaneous reply was, "No sir, Son, we're turning around *today* and going home. Our revival starts Sunday, and we're not about to go to any New York. Either you head your car home, or I'll catch a bus!" "Well, no," I said, "You don't need to do that."

On the way home, we did stop by the biggest apple storage facility in the U.S.—and maybe in the world—in Wheeling, West Virginia. Again, in the Shenandoah Valley, we feasted our eyes on palatial homes with large front lawns, some with calves or horses grazing in them, and perhaps large natural stones left as landscape features.

But all the way back Papa kept saying, "We want to be *sure* we can get back by Sunday." And we did.

World War II

My son, Robert Hunt II, was born on December 5, 1941. Two or three days later I went to Milan Hospital to see him and Lillie May. A radio was on, and we heard the announcement: "Pearl

Harbor has been bombed." I said, "We are in for war!" Later the same day, they got to relating how many were killed, how many ships were destroyed, and how many suicide bombers came in.

Soon we heard President Roosevelt speaking of the infamy of the attack, saying that no nation could take such an offense, and that we would declare war. Dr. Stewart was conscripted and served in the Pacific. He saw so much death and carnage in Iwo Jima that he gave up surgery and went into pediatrics. However, the government notified me: "You remain in the town where you are unless we call you to go somewhere else. We'll expect you to examine drafted individuals to see if they are fit for the Service." So that's what I did, and some of those who went to the war later ribbed me, "By the way, you're the one who put me in the Army!" They had wanted me to disqualify them, but I had said, "Yeah, you're physically fit."

A few veterans tried to get pensions after the war, and I had to examine them to see if they qualified for disability pensions. Several times, after examining a man, I sent in a report that I didn't find anything seriously wrong with him. He then would go to another doctor, who would also turn him down. Then he'd tell me, "Now, you kept me from getting my pension because you said I was in sound condition, but you *know* I've got this problem!"

Besides examining draftees, I served the government by examining employees for the Arsenal and the Illinois Central Railroad by examining their employees and treating some of them. I was given a free pass on the Illinois Central, but never really took advantage of it except for a few trips to Memphis. Today I hold several service certificates from the government and one from the I.C. Railroad.

Trips elsewhere

Other than going to Washington, D.C., with my daddy, I've made only a few extensive trips. Once Trebor, Sue Gowan, and I drove out to San Diego together in Sue's car, stopping on the way to visit the Petrified Forest and the Grand Canyon.

After reaching San Diego, we drove down to the Mexican border and crossed over for a brief visit in Tijuana. This is the only time in my life that I've been outside of the U.S.A.

After a week in San Diego, Trebor and I left Sue there, boarding the train for our return trip home. The train went north to Los Angeles before heading east. We had to travel all night, and there were only soldiers on the train besides us. I said, "Lord have mercy!" They were going up and down the aisle all night, and we couldn't get any rest. Well, I notified Lillie May as to when I thought we'd be arriving back in Memphis. But when we got to Amarillo, Texas, we had a two-hour layover. Dr. "Foetus" [= fetus] Johnson had been in my medical class, and I knew he was practicing there. So I called him on the phone, and he picked us up and carried us over to his home, an old house that he had remodeled. He had such a view that you could see flat land for miles around. We stayed and talked a while, then returned to the train, which passed through Little Rock and finally reached Memphis.

Since I had phoned ahead, Roy Laster had driven Lillie May down to meet our train. But we had figured the schedule wrong, and didn't arrive until the day after I had told her we would. So when we got to Memphis we waited and waited, but no one came for us. Then, phoning Medina, we found out that they had come for us the day before. I moaned, "We made a mistake in timing!" So we had to catch a bus and come home. But you talk about a worn-out pair! . . .

Lillie May and I did take one more trip,[2] with Dr. and Mrs. Steven Byars, in the early Seventies. We went from here up to Des Moines, Iowa, then through Omaha, Nebraska, through Kansas, and over to Yellowstone National Park, staying there several days. It was a good trip.

Now I'm like Paul Gowan: I feel there ought to be a law that says a man can't get out of his county. There's too much traffic on the road, and there are too many deaths. Paul says, "I don't need to go anywhere; it's too dangerous, getting killed on the highway."

CHAPTER XIV
HOME LIFE

How I see my wife

A year or two after we moved to Medina, Lillie May became a charter member of the Church of Christ that was being formed. This was hard for me to accept, and has been a source of friction in our marriage. At one time I considered leaving her, but thought, *No, I can't do that*. I told my daddy, "I just can't carry on with the different beliefs, and I'm just so disturbed about it." But he said, "Nooooo, can't think about nothing like that!"

But I'm learning to love my wife more and more every day. I can say this for her: We married the day that she finished her nurse's training and I my internship, and we began practice together. No man could have married a woman with more patience or more endurance, and no woman could have been more encouraging and more true to her husband than Lillie May. No one could have done a better job of caring for my home, putting up with the demands of my practice, answering the phone all the time. She kept house with five children, and with all the neighbors' children coming over here to play. I'd come home and hear the kids rolling or jumping upstairs, and I'd say, "Lillie May, they're going to break the ceiling in!" But she'd answer, "Well, I know where they are." And she did all the sewing for the children, and dressed them so neat and pretty. I'd be grouchy, coming in late, tired, and worried, but she'd always be pleasant. You could ask anyone who called on her for help; Lillie May did her best.

She was good to the children, and I can add this: She was always at home. Whenever I'd be gone on a call, or maybe not come in all night, she was there for the children, and for me when I got home. I really can't say enough about her; I could kiss her every day. I don't know how to express my love and appreciation for her adequately.

The only negative I see in her (if it *is* a negative) is that she'd give away everything we've got if I'd let her. She'll give you anything she's got if you say that you need it. No one who came to our door—black or white, a hobo or a schoolchild—was turned away empty-handed.

And she was very supportive in my practice. If patients came to the house, and she knew that I was gone, she would do what she could for them. In fact, she was very capable of acting to meet their needs, even in serious cases like convulsions. She'd give them first aid, then send them to the hospital if they needed to go. The schoolyard is behind our house, and teachers sometimes sent school children here for first aid.

Three or four years ago, the Western boy[1] came up here at my request. Lightning had burned out my antenna booster, and I wanted him to put in another one. (He works in the utility department of the city of Milan.) He came, climbed this long antenna that I had up, and put the new booster in. When he came back inside, I asked him what it would cost, but he didn't say.

Two or three months passed, then one day he showed up at our door. I opened the door and, after greeting him, said, "How much do I owe you?" "Where is your wife? She's back there in the back room." "I want her to come in here.… I want to tell you something: I'm not going to charge you anything for putting in this booster. But your wife—I've never forgotten it since I was a six-year-old kid: Mrs. Virgie Morse brought me over here. I had soiled my pants; I was dirty and nasty. Your wife took me out there in the well-house with a tub of warm water, and cleaned me up, and got some of your son Robert's clothes and put them on me, and sent me home clean. I brought the clothes back the next day, but I have never forgotten that incident to this day. Now Doc, you take her out and treat her and Mrs. Virgie to the best meal you can give them, and if I hear you don't do it, you owe me $107 for putting in this booster. But if you'll feed them like I tell you to, you won't owe me a thing. I want your wife to know that I'm up in years now [40-something], but I have never forgotten it."

Lillie May would do that for any of them. I've seen her give away her oil paintings, worth I don't know how many dollars, even after getting them framed. I tell her, "If you're going to do something momentous, you'd better just buy something and give it to them!"

A bemused Dr. Morris observes wife Lillie May with one of her paintings, 1970. This photo appeared in a Sunday edition of the *Jackson Sun* (Jackson, Tenn.); it was taken at the Harvest Years Center by a *Sun* photographer.

We share a faith in Jesus as the Son of God and our Savior, and we both believe the Scriptures to be inspired by God and our authority for faith and practice. But I contend that we must look to Jesus alone for our salvation, and not look to any acts we perform as helping secure it. If we look to these things—Paul says, "If circumcision means anything, Christ is of no avail."[2] In particular, we differ in our understanding of the purpose of baptism. Still, we can pray together, love each other, and forgive when we've hurt each other, we and our children.

Our children

I've already mentioned the births of our children—four girls and one boy:

Una Deane, born October 31, 1936, at home in Gibson, attended by Dr. Rozzell;

Trebor Morton, born July 4, 1938, at our first home in Medina, with Dr. Weldon Oliver assisting me in delivery;

Brenda Leake, born May 20, 1940, at our present home in Medina, with Dr. Steven Byars attending;

Robert Hunt, born December 5, 1941, in Clemmer Clinic (now Milan Hospital), delivered by Dr. Henry Moore; and

Lillie Katherine, born November 11, 1944, at Doctors' Hospital in Jackson, delivered by Dr. John Pierce.

We were fortunate that our lot adjoined the school campus. Every one of my children attended Medina schools all 12 years. They could, and usually did, come home for lunch; school never kept us from leading a normal family life. I knew where they were. If anything happened to them, they could come right home. Many an evening we would all be in our living room; I'd be reading, Lillie May either reading or knitting, and the children doing homework. Usually we'd all be quiet at least part of the time. We had no TV until the mid-fifties.

Sometimes we'd read stories together such as *Bird Life in Wington*. At one time Sammy Campbell, our basketball coach, and at another time Rosalind Taylor, our home economics teacher, lived with us. We attended our church services three times a week and our home basketball games; occasionally our children went to the picture show. On Sunday afternoons we might go to Gibson to see Papa and other members of my family.

Other neighborhood children, especially the Graves and Stubblefield boys, often played in our house with our own children.

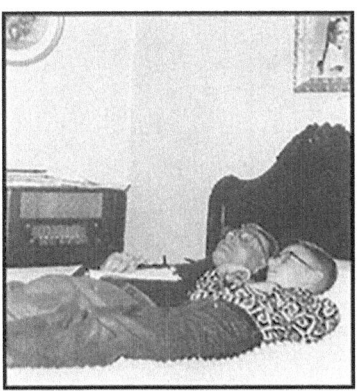

On reverse: "Daddy and Robert Hunt lounging. 1953. Being up at night, Daddy often rests at noon—till phone rings."

All our children did well in school. Trebor, Brenda, and Robert were valedictorians of their classes. All did well in college, and none had serious academic trouble. A professor at Union University said that Trebor was one of the 10 best students he had ever taught in math.

I kept up a number of magazine subscriptions: *Saturday Evening Post, Look, Life, Reader's Digest, National Geographic*, various children's magazines, and religious literature. I also filled our home with books, including *The Harvard Classics*, encyclopedias, sets on nature and history, and so on. My children had access to all kinds of literature that I thought was good, sound reading. I wouldn't buy trash. The reason I waited so long to get a TV was that I didn't want my children distracted from their studies.

In high school, Una was a cheerleader; Trebor and Brenda played basketball; Robert was statistician one year but never played; and Lillie was a cheerleader her freshman year and a statistician the next three.

Portrait of the Robert Morris family in 1946, by McCauley's Studio, Jackson, Tenn. In the middle row, left *to right:* Una, Brenda, and Trebor; Brenda is holding Lillie.

Left: Five children with Dad on swing set, Nov. 1, 1946. Perched on top, *l. to r.:* Brenda, Una, and Trebor. *Right:* The five children ready for church on a Sunday morning, 1949. Una, Trebor, and Brenda stand *l. to r.* behind Robert and Lillie.

All five children obtained bachelor degrees in college. Una attended the University of Tennessee at Martin. When she first left home for college I told her, "Hon, we're just now beginning to make our final step for the breakup of our home." At UT-Martin Una met Craig Grant, whom she married after graduation. Trebor went one year to UT-Martin, then transferred to Union University and finished there because that is where her future husband, Melton Ambrose, was enrolled. Brenda attended Freed- Hardeman College two years, and later, UT-Martin, where she graduated. Robert Hunt attended and graduated from Southwestern at Memphis (later renamed Rhodes College). Lillie Katherine had her four years at UT-Martin.[3]

I feel justified in having had a certain pride in my children. I would look at those little children; I'd see Lillie May dressing those four little girls and one boy. I thought they were some of the finest children in the world, and as far as *I* am concerned, they *were*.

As a boy, Robert Hunt never talked back to me. Whenever I asked him to do something, like: "Robert, will you go and cut some weeds?" he'd say, "All right, Daddy"; and he'd have it done when I got home. After his year away in France, we did have arguments, but that's all behind us now.

I never had any trouble with my girls growing up, either. They all did their own studying and made good in high school. The only thing that has caused me concern over the years has been some problems in their marriages, but all are doing reasonably well today.

An incident remembered by Roz (Taylor) Davis

The following was included in a letter to Trebor Ambrose dated January 28, 1991, after Roz learned of Dr. Morris's death. Rosalind roomed and boarded with the Morrises in 1959 while teaching home economics in Medina High School. She has remained a friend of the family ever since.)

You and Melton were newly-weds and lived in the upstairs room. I shared a room with Lillie Katherine, who was also my student. It was a Sunday afternoon when I moved in. Bright and early Monday morning, Dr. Morris was in the center hall in his underwear, shaving. He made enough noise to wake the whole house. After supper that night, he invited me into the living room for some TV watching. There was also a ball game that night. Lillie was a cheerleader and Robert Hunt kept stats. Neither had to pay to get into the game. Just before leaving for the ball game, both Lillie and Robert came and knelt at the Doctor's knees.[4] *Then they proceeded to beg him for 10 cents each, so they could have a soda at the game. He gave them to believe that it was unnecessary for them to have that, and he mumbled and grumbled quite a bit before he gave them the money. Both ran out the back door and over to the gym, like a streak of lightning. When they were gone, he turned to me and said, "What'd ya think of that?" I said, "I didn't think much of it. You should have given them more than that. After all, you didn't have to pay anything for them to get in." After that, I thought he would tell me to re-pack my bags and get out! To my surprise, he looked me straight in the eye and said, "Well...you're all right, long, tall one. You say what you think." We always got along really well after that.*

A portrait of the Robert Morris family in March, 1951. Here Una is 14, Trebor 12, Brenda almost 11, Robert nine, and Lillie six. Made by Leemans Studio, Jackson, Tenn.

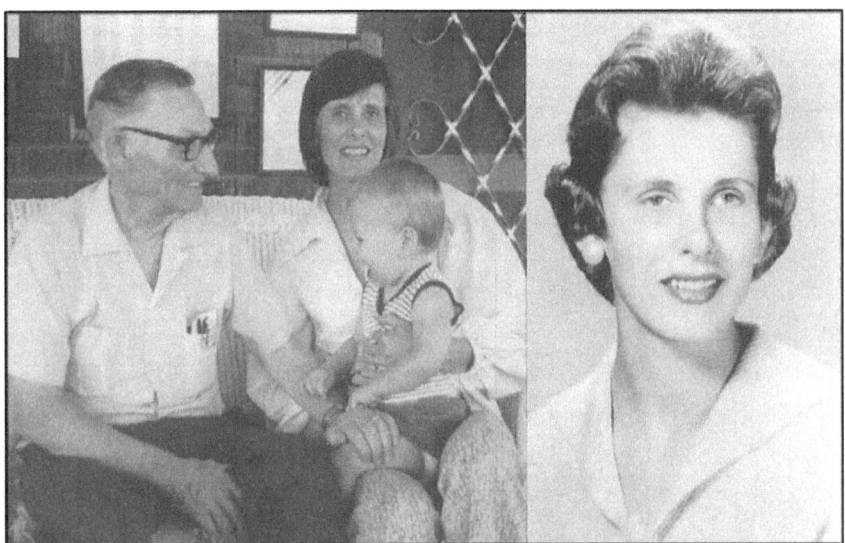

Left: Dr. Morris with Rosalind (Taylor) Davis and her son Kevin on the porch of the Morris home, 1976. After rooming and boarding in the Morris home in 1959–60, Roz became a lifelong friend. *Right:* Roz in 1960, when she taught home economics at Medina High School and lived with the Morrises.

CHAPTER XV

RETIREMENT

In my practice, I never felt like I could keep up with all the demands placed on me. Often people came to our home after hours when they were off work or had emergencies. The phone frequently woke me up during the night, and I'd have to go on a call, sometimes 'way out in the country. It was hard to close the office early on Saturday afternoons like I wanted to; however, in my last few years of practice I was more successful at doing so. All too often, when I got out of church around noon on Sunday, someone would be waiting for me, saying, "Doctor, I came to see you today, because during the week I'm busy and don't have the time. I wonder if you'd go over to the office and examine me?" This constant drain on my time and energy became one factor making me long for retirement.

Still, except for dropping obstetrics, which involved so many night calls, I took few vacations and kept going at a pretty hard pace until health problems forced me to slow down. I think that having a simple style of life —medical practice, family, church, gardening, yard work, medical meetings, and TV—helped me keep going so long. It wasn't easy to slow down, with OB patients pleading, insisting, even getting mad. I'd say, "Honey, I just *can't* do it. I'm quitting, and if I'm going to quit, I've got to *quit!*"

Another factor making practice more difficult and less rewarding was the government stepping in with Medicare and Medicaid. During my first 20 years of practice, I hardly ever saw a patient with health insurance. Then some of the blacks began carrying policies, paying something like 25 cents a week premium to an agent who regularly collected from them. When they came to me, they would ask me to fill out a form for everything I did, so they could get reimbursed.

Later came Medicare. As I recall, when this program was first introduced, the patient's deductible was either $240 or $250 per year. Let's say that I would see the patient two or three times and that he would pay me. Then, for whatever reason, he would go to the hospital, where they would require him to pay his initial $250. Once he had done that, they would tell him that he was entitled to 80% reimbursement of all other medical bills incurred that year. So the patient would come back to me and demand a refund of money he had paid me.

This was time-consuming, because my books were set up as a daily log of cash receipts, along with individual charge accounts. If he had paid cash, but could not tell me the exact dates he had seen me, I would have to search back through my daily log. Having done that, I would have to fill out the Medicare form, then wait a number of weeks to get my 80% from the government, and still have to ask the patient for the other 20%. Such practices annoyed me to the point that I said, "Lillie May, if I've got to do this, I'll quit. I *cannot* put up with such stuff! Otherwise, I will have to hire an insurance secretary to keep records of every call and help me with the forms so we can get this information immediately when we need it."

For the little I charged, and with the heavy load I carried, I felt all this paperwork would destroy me, so I just closed my doors. Nowadays most doctors do have insurance secretaries who fill out the forms for them. Others post on their door, MEDICARE NOT ACCEPTED; they don't want to fool with it.

Major surgery

In 1966, I noticed that my feet and legs were burning and stinging. Then one day I felt in my groin and said, "Hmm! I can hardly get a pulse!" I told Roy Graves, "I'll bet you I'm *in* for it!" When I told my son-in-law, Craig Grant, a neurosurgeon, what was going on, he said, "You'd better do something about it, or you're gonna have *real* trouble. You ought to go out to DeBakey Clinic in Houston." Trebor and Melton Ambrose were living in Houston at that time. Dr. DeBakey, for whom the clinic was named, was the famous pioneer in vascular surgery. The clinic was part of the Methodist Hospital.

So I talked with my son-in-law, Dr. Ambrose, who made an appointment for me to go out there. I thought I would see DeBakey. However, when I got to the clinic, I was sent to Dr. E. Stanley Crawford, who had trained under Dr. DeBakey and supposedly was the main man there in blood vessels.

Lillie May and I went out in early November 1966, and Melton and Trebor took me to the hospital, where I was admitted for a workup. One morning technicians came in, saying they had to do an arteriogram of my neck. I said, "Am I the right patient? My trouble's all in my groin!" They double-checked, then proceeded with the arteriogram and found out that I had partial blockage in the aorta and the iliac arteries.

The next day Dr. Crawford came in and said, "Yeah, I know what you've got, and it's going to require surgery." I said, "Doctor, I don't really feel sick. Do you think it's necessary?" "Do you want to lose your legs?" "No sir, I don't." "Well, you've got to have something done, and you'd better do it now." "Well, I guess I'll just have to surrender to an operation." "All right, we'll get you tomorrow."

So that night I was prepared for surgery, and the following day, November 8th, a shuttle-bus came to take me to the main hospital. I was taken downstairs, where they gave me a shot, then rolled me on a stretcher into the elevator and took me upstairs, leaving me in the hallway outside the operating room. While waiting, I looked around and said, "My golly! The vastness of this place! And look at that operating room; I never saw so much equipment!" The anesthetist came by in a minute and said, "Let me have your hand; I want a vein." I said, "Uh-oh, he's getting ready to give me sodium pentathol." He stuck me, and I began counting. When I got to 10 or 11, it was like a light going out.

When I woke up, I was down in intensive care, which was in a big open room. I said, "Oh, Lord, my stomach is burning up! This is burning me *so* bad!" They gave me another shot and knocked me out. After I roused a second time, I noticed a woman on one side of me smothering to death under an oxygen tent, and on the other a man who said his name was Kittican, an Armenian living in California. He told me how the Turks massacred Armenians and how they felt toward the Turks.

I received an operation called an endarterectomy, intended to clean out my abdominal aorta and the arteries to my legs without a transplant. But 48 hours after the operation, I noted with alarm the dark color of my foot and said, "Dr. Crawford, look here!" He said, "Some of that 'rock' [calcium from blood vessel wall] has gotten in your foot; you've got an embolus." Then he added, "If collateral circulation doesn't take care of it, you'll lose your foot." I said, "Oh my!"

So while I was there, I kept watching this foot. I had these big tension sutures in my abdomen; I was cut from my sternum (breast-bone) to my pubic symphysis. They had even gone down into my groins. Melton observed the operation, and said "I've never seen so much taken out of a blood vessel."

That foot continued bothering me for some time, and, when I was discharged from the hospital, I spent several more weeks in the home of Melton and Trebor. I had to go back to the clinic to have the tension sutures taken out before leaving for Tennessee.

It was following this operation that I began seriously cutting back in my practice.

Dr. Robert H. Morris Appreciation Day

I guess it was when I came back from Houston that some of the people in Medina began to plan an appreciation day for me. It was supposed to be a secret, but I became aware of it one or two days before it actually took place on a Sunday afternoon in June, 1967. In spite of the heat, the gymnasium where the activities were held was almost full. Achele Parrett, Betty Coleman, Evelyn Barnes, and Rebecca Graves sang, accompanied by Edna Bradbury on piano. The gym floor was covered with tables, and a dinner was served. Our mayor, Moody Mills, made some introductory remarks. Then Mike Champlin, my former pastor at the First Baptist Church who had gone on to a large church in Memphis, spoke. He described my character with a lot of humor; for example, sitting in my office chair, with my feet on the examining table, reading my medical journal. My dad, then 85 and with only a few weeks to live, made a few remarks in a feeble voice, like, "Robert has always been a good boy and worked hard." Our son Robert Hunt had come from New York,[1] and he, Una and her husband

Craig, and Lillie Katherine, sat at the table of honor with Lillie May, Papa, and myself. (Trebor and Brenda were unable to attend.)

Then they called on me, and I said a few things extemporaneously. I told them about coming to Medina, and so on, and remember ending with: "I guess I'll go on till the curtain comes down." Some men had taken up a collection and presented me with a big color TV. (George Arthur Parrish also gave me a suit that I like to wear and that is in my closet now.)

Of course, the Appreciation Day gave me a sense of satisfaction. I had tried to serve the community, and people believed they could depend on me. They'd say, "Well, if he tells you it's so-and-so, that's it!" I'd tell them yes or no or, if I wasn't sure of a diagnosis, I'd say, "I *don't* know what's wrong with you, but I'm afraid it may be this. I'm going to send you to a specialist." Sometimes I'd tell them, "I don't care what they say; I believe you've got this. You can go to someone else if you want to; or, if you let me, I'll send you to someone I recommend. I'd rather you go to Memphis to (let's say) Dr. Tom West with what I think you've got."

Dr. Robert Morris Appreciation Day, June 11, 1967, held in Medina High School gymnasium (no air-conditioning!). Seated at table of honor *(from left):* Una and Craig Grant, Lillie Katherine, Mrs. Morris, and Dr. Morris, half-standing, who is speaking with an unidentified woman. In foreground, Dr. Morris's father, Joe Morris, is speaking to Winifred Dobbins (cousin of Lillie May Morris).

Papa's death

My father, Joseph Edward Morris, died on July 19, 1967, at the age of 85. Guy and Sue had cared for Papa during the last few years of his life. Toward the end he would struggle to get out of bed; he also would get disoriented as to time and place. He would go to bed at 8 p.m., then, when Guy went to bed at 10 p.m., Papa would want to get up. Guy and Sue would say, "Papa, it's time to go to bed!" But he'd already been in bed, and now he wasn't sleepy.

During this period, Papa was a handful for Guy and Sue. On Wednesdays he might dress for Sunday church. One time he got outside and climbed onto the fence, and Sue was unable to get him off; she had to call for some children on the school playground across the street to help her. Sue cared for Papa with an unusual degree of patience and kindness. Papa, during this period, would refuse whenever I urged him to spend the night at our home in Medina, no matter how late it was. I'd beg him to stay but he'd say, "I've got to go home."

As Papa grew weaker, he had more and more difficulty getting off the bed, and would just lie there, breathing. We considered hospitalization, but I said, "I'm not going to carry him there and put all kinds of intravenouses in him; I'll let him alone." And in a few days, he died peacefully.

Further health problems

I had an operation on my prostate in 1970, then my foot had an embolus soon afterward, and it hurt me all the time. It was burning, stinging, and cold. Finally I got in such a state that I said, "It looks like I just can't put up with this discomfort." So I closed my office that year;[2] I was 65 years old, almost 66.

I began drawing Social Security, having become eligible to participate only in the last five or six years of my practice, since before that time, self- employed professionals were excluded unless incorporated. My first check was 92 dollars. Some of my colleagues in Jackson had been smart to incorporate years before, which allowed them to participate earlier than I did. One doctor told me he was drawing $20,000 per year on Social Security. When I asked how that happened, he said he just kept paying into it until he was 70 or more.

I asked our friend Herschel Cooley, who recently retired as director of the Social Security office in Jackson, about this. He confirmed the doctor's story—he knew a lawyer who kept paying until he was 70. Most people, however, draw $500 to $700 per month.

One day in 1977 I fell out in the garden, with pain in my hip and leg. I practically had to be dragged from the garden, because I couldn't help myself. I went to Jackson to see Dr. Erb, who sent me on to Memphis. There Dr. Crosby did an arteriogram on me, then said he would operate the next day. This he did, creating a bypass from the right subclavian artery to the femorals in my leg—from my upper chest to my groin—then grafting across my symphysis into my left leg.

When I woke up, I found out I had received the same operation that I had seen performed a year earlier on Cora Sims' husband. I thought, *My golly, how traumatic this is!* The following day, I woke up only to find that all over my chest, side, and back, as well as in my groins and upper legs, the blood had extravasated (oozed out of the vessels) under the skin and fascia. It hurt me to cough or sneeze, to take a deep breath, or to move my body. Dr. Crosby hadn't told me that this was what he was going to do.

Celebrating Dr. Morris's seventieth birthday in September 1974: Laura Bell Moore, Robert Hunt (II), and Dr. and Mrs. Morris. Robert made a surprise visit from North Carolina. Laura Bell (1914–1976) had been employed in the Morris home for a number of years, and came to help on this special occasion. Dr. Morris had co-signed the note for her house when she was unable to obtain a mortgage loan otherwise. She lived to pay it off, and their friendship continued until her death.

When first released from the hospital, I stayed on in Memphis with Lillie May's cousin, Louise Morton, for a few days; then I went on home. While lying in bed one night, after about two weeks at home, I felt for a pulse in my groin and told Lillie May, "I don't have a pulse! This operation was of no avail."

I went back down to Memphis to see Dr. Crosby, but he wasn't in, and I saw his associate, Dr. Harrington, instead. After hearing my complaint, Dr. Harrington took out his amplifiers and listened carefully, then said, "Well, I don't get much pulse either. Why did you get this operation?" I replied, "I don't know. I woke up with it! But, Doctor, if you're asking me why it was ever done, I won't be back." And I never went back to him or Crosby.

Seven grandchildren help Dr. Morris to celebrate his 75th birthday in 1979. These are *(left to right):* Richie Ambrose, Jill Nulter (John Robert Ambrose is in front of her), Christy Cate, Kelly Nulter, Tom Cate, Bryant Nulter. The Medina school is in the background.

A stroke

In 1981, while teaching a Sunday School class, I noticed a little tingling in my hands. This sensation passed, and the days went by without anything unusual until, one morning, when I was sitting in my easy chair, my arm began tingling, then became paralyzed. I called Lillie May and said, "I can't move my arm. Try handling it." And it was as limp as a rag. About 10 or 11 o'clock the feeling came back and I could work my hand a little. I said, "I wonder if something is blocked in me, in my carotid."

I went to Dr. George Thomas in Jackson, who, after examining me, said, "You're getting ready for a good stroke; you'll have to have something done." They did an arteriogram, going in under my arm. The technician doing the procedure said, "I never put one under the arm before." But they were afraid to use the artery in my groin, as they'd gone in there so many times already. The technician reported: "Yeah, your carotid is blocked on the right side, nearly closed off, and the left side is blocked some." So Dr. Thomas said, "I'd operate, if I was you." "Well, I'll go home and cut my yard and be back." So that's what I did, and he cleaned out my right carotid.

In '83 I went to Jackson Clinic. They said I had a stricture in my femoral artery, and they were going to go in and dilate it. When they went in to do this, Dr. Alexander, the head of the X-ray department who was to do the procedure, told me I was the 120th or 130th patient he had dilated. He claimed that none of his patients had had complications with the procedure, and that he had performed it on two old men that morning before me. They went in my groin, put this instrument through, and brought it over to the stricture in my left femoral. Dr. Alexander said, "Bob, I'm going to blow this balloon up and stretch this stricture, and after I break that plaque in there, I'll take it out. When the artery begins to stretch, it stings a little. When it starts stinging, tell me and I'll stop."

So he proceeded with the dilatation until I said, "Dr. Alexander, it's gone to stinging, burning!" "All right, I'll stop." Then 10 or 15 seconds later I said, "Dr. Alexander, it's getting awful!" And a moment later: "It's getting outrageous; I can't stand it!" Then he got busy. I said, "It's going to *kill* me!" He had ruptured my left femoral artery below the groin, and in a few more minutes I would have bled to death. I was hollering at the top of my voice, and I was begging the Lord, "Oh Lord, don't let me die! Please don't! Don't let me die!"

They were rushing around me now, and got Lillie May to come in and sign for surgery. Meanwhile they were taking me all the way from the X-ray room in the basement to the second floor, and setting up to operate. While they were still preparing, I went into shock from loss of blood. They gave me seven pints, and Dr. Thomas later told my brother John, "You'll never know how near your brother came to dying." I think they had to resuscitate me three times while trying to get blood back in me, since I had lost so much. Thomas went in and stopped the bleeding, and grafted a vessel across my pubic symphysis into the left femoral. This graft proved to be more successful than the earlier one, and I still have some circulation, however weak, in my left leg.

But my problems weren't over: After that, the heel and toes of my left foot turned dark and blistered up. I spent some time in the home of our youngest daughter, Lillie Cate, in Paris, Tennessee, because Lillie May just couldn't take care of me like I needed. Lillie Katherine took me back to the doctor, and when Hubbard saw my foot he said. "Bob, you're going to have to have it cut off." I said, "Well, it looks like I'm either going to have to do that or lose my toes." But Dr. Thomas said, "Well, you just wait; I've seen a lot of people come out of this."

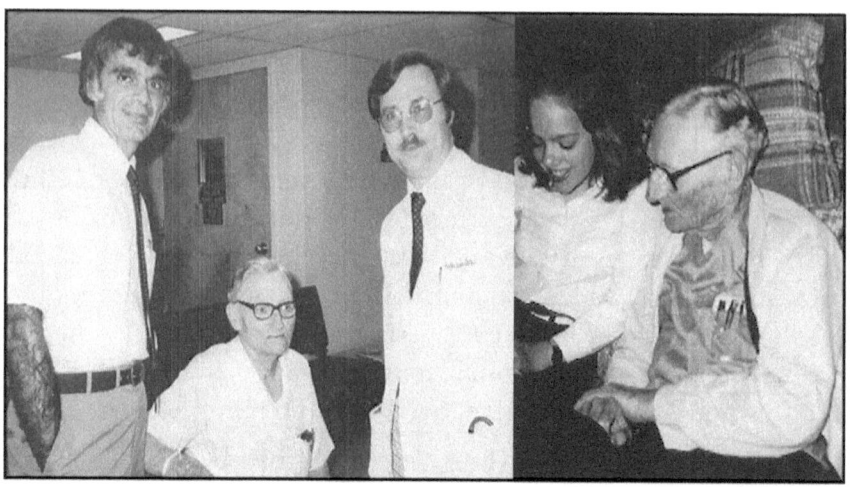

Left: Dr. Morris as a patient, between Dr. George Thomas, L, his vascular surgeon, and Dr. Shaw, R, who performed his second prostate operation. Dr. Morris remembered both these operations as being in 1981, but this photograph bears the date "Sept. 1982." *Right:* Dr. Morris with granddaughter Christy Cate, here holding a hymnal, during his recovery from vascular surgery when he stayed in the Cate home in Paris, Tenn, for 4½ months. Photo bears the date of April 1982.

So I stayed with the Cates—Lillie, Charles, Tom, and Christy—four and a half months, and they took good care of me. Then the skin sloughed off of my toe; I could feel the bone, and the heel was dark, almost black. It was pitiful what I went through those four months. But in spite of the pain and discomfort, I was afraid to take pain medication, knowing I could easily become addicted to it. So I'd lie there at night, looking at the ceiling, and would still be looking at that ceiling the next morning, not having slept a wink. I couldn't get my sock on, and I couldn't get a shoe big enough to wear without hurting my toes.

Gradually, however, my foot began to heal some, and I returned to Medina. I remember walking around the house, putting my heel down and hopping because of those toes. They had great big blisters and looked awful. But I'm using those toes today, even though they still burn or feel cold, and sting all the time. The discomfort keeps me in a restless state; I can't get comfortable. Also, when I get up to walk, I easily lose my balance.

In 1981 I had a second prostate operation, following the first in 1970. I went to Jackson Clinic to see Dr. Stauffer, who had been caring for me. He said, "Bob, with your prostate growing again and your small stream, you'd best be operated on. Then you'll have an open flow." "What about you doing it?" "No, I quit yesterday." "You mean you wouldn't operate a-tall?" "No, I'm done; I quit." "Well, who would you get?" And he said, "Shaw's all right." "Well," I said, "I guess I'll get him, then." Following that operation, however, I've had a stricture ever since. I have to go to the clinic every four to six months to be dilated, and it hurts me terribly.

Portrait of Dr. & Mrs. Robert Morris, made for their fiftieth wedding anniversary (Dec. 31, 1985). This picture appeared in *The Mirror-Exchange* (Milan, Tenn.) on Jan. 29, 1986.

Gathering at the Cate home in Paris, Tenn., to celebrate "Papaw"'s 83rd birthday, 1987. *Left to right:* Una Grant, Trebor Ambrose, Brenda Nulter, Dr. and Mrs. Morris, Robert Morris II, and Lillie Cate. Photo by Charles Cate.

Distinguished alumnus

A pleasant surprise, more recently, was being named a distinguished alumnus of Union University. This occurred at their 1985 Homecoming banquet, and I was presented with a Distinguished Service Award. When they invited me to make some remarks, I really cut loose, and they had a hard time shutting me up. Old Stewart, fundraiser for the university, politely interrupted saying, "Well, is that all?," and I said, "Well, as soon as I finish this." But when it was over, old Bro. Brashear, now down in Mobile, Alabama, said, "I have never heard anything like that before in my life. That's the beatingest story I've ever heard!" And all of them who spoke to me said, "Well, I've never heard anything like that!"

Honored by Medina First Baptist Church

RMII: In early 1990 Dad was slightly injured in an automobile accident and began having other physical difficulties. Already he had resigned as Sunday School teacher, and after this accident he resigned as deacon. The church accepted his resignation while naming him Deacon Emeritus and, without his knowing it but with his wife's cooperation, began planning an appreciation day. This took place on Sunday, April 1, 1990, in what began as a regular church service. In the fall of 1990, I wrote Dad, asking him to send me a report on the appreciation day. What follows is the contents of a letter dated "11-17-90," written in Dr. Morris's own hand, less than a week before he first entered the hospital with his final illness. It is the only significant portion of this book that Dr. Morris actually wrote, rather than narrating on tape, and it was his final contribution except for answering a couple of questions for me during his final hospitalization. I have preserved original spelling and punctuation, and have indicated corrections in brackets. The handwriting is impressively even and strong, in spite of Dr. Morris's age and poor health.

Special cake made for Dr. Morris's 85th birthday by Helen (Blackshire) Jones. Each layer recorded a stage in the doctor's life.

Dear Son:

You requested a report of the services in our church, 1st Baptist to honor me 4-1-90

The service had been kept a complete secret from me[;] I was in total darkness.

I went to church[,] looked at Program[. It] did not give What Bro. Gay was to preach[;] thought I had wrong program but dated 4- 1-90. Evelyn Key my sister came in, I greeted her but was surprised at her visit but did not [ask, "]Why are you here[?"] Then Bro. John Pippin, wife and daughter came in[.] I greeted them and I surmised he was to preach that day. Then Guy [Morris, my brother] came in[.] I greeted him, first thought he came for me to see Sue, but invited him to our class and he came over. Soon [your] Mother, Charles Cate, Lillie K and and Christy came in to our class. I was confused[;] they all stayed in class until lesson was over. I asked Bobby Don Harris to go tell Bro. Gay to invite Bro. Pippin to preach the Morning Service. He did not return, soon Bro. Gay came in announcing the purpose of the morning service, would be to honor Dr. Robert Morris for his service in the church during past 50 or more years. I was nearly in shock. I was called and family to front seat. Later Melton & Trebor came in. Little later Dr Lamb Myhr came in and took a seat in back which I did not know.

Medina Baptist Church building, where, on April 1, 1990, Dr. Morris was honored in a special service for his 50 years as a deacon and Sunday School teacher.

After song service and Prayer a video was shown and Dr. Myrham [Hiram] Barefoot came on a[nd] gave remarks about a graduate of U[nion] U[niversity]. I attended services at Union of[t]en and stated that UU honored me with special award 5 yrs ago for Human ser[v]ices over the past yr[s] and a Plaque so stating.

Next Dr Lamb Myhr was called to the Podium to speak, [I] not knowing he was present and he came forward stating he had known me 40 year[s]—how I had served in the Medical profession, wanting the best for my patients, and Dr Leland Johnston said when [Bob Morris] sends one in[,] put [the patient] in the Hosp[ital], [Bob's] diagnosis was good. He last stated he [was] asked a few days past[, "W]hat do you think of Bob Morris[?" His answer was, "]He trys [sic] to keep up to date[,] attends meetings consistently[,] and He is known for His Honesty."

First page of the letter Dr. Morris wrote his son Robert on Nov. 17, 1990, less than six weeks before his death. The handwriting is impressively even and strong.

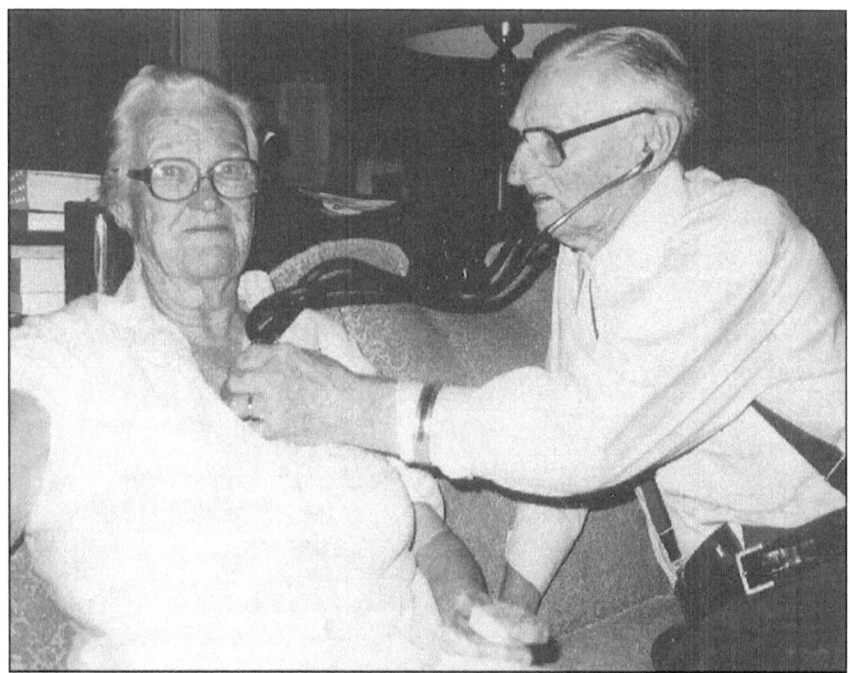

Dr. Morris examining Olive Hinson, Dec. 1988. Following official retirement, he continued to examine patients, give shots, and write prescriptions at home until his final illness. Olive Hinson, a registered nurse and a resident of Medina, was the first night supervisor of nurses in Jackson-Madison County General Hospital (now called Jackson General). Photo by LLM.

Then Bro Pippin was called to speak[.] He re[s]tated our services [together] over the 13 yrs [while] he was Pastor..., our love for each other[,] some of my characteristics[,] and [a] few close experiences c³ me during those yrs.

Next Mr. William Eddings[,] chairman of Board of Deacon[s:] He said many things about my services and called me to the podium and presented me with a Plaque stating my 52 yrs as a deacon and 51 yrs as a teacher of the men[']s class. I received the Plaque[;] I tried to respond[,] telling of my past[,] stating raised by Godly parents—my struggle getting through Medical School internship, why coming to Medina and how—some [of] my experiences there and my love for the Medina 1st Baptist Church.

Then Bro. Gay invited all into the educational Bldg. to a bountiful meal and the ladies of the church had prepared a variety of foods, well prepared and a bountiful supply. After the meal the services were over. John and Johnny [L]eake were there. After the meal we departed to our homes.

I am tired will stop. All in all a great day.
I hope this gives you some idea of the service
May the [Lord] keep and direct you.

Love Dad

PS - Bro Williams [William] Eddings related the remarks you phoned to his Home.

Written remarks from Brenda were read.
A good video was taken by Charles Studdard.

PART II

INCIDENTS, OBSERVATIONS, AND RELATIONS

CHAPTER XVI

INCIDENTS IN MY PRACTICE

What's good for the cow...?

Once I got a phone call from the family of old man McClain on Law Road: "Come quick, Doctor; he's having a stroke!" When I got there, Mr. McClain was having convulsions. After watching him a while, I said, "No, you haven't had a stroke, but have you been taking any medicine lately?" "Well, yeah, I took a tablet from that box there." I ordered the family, "Get it and let me see." Someone handed the box to me, and I read what was on the top. "What does this word cow on it mean?" "Oh, golly bill, I took one of those cow pills—strychnine!" Then it hit me: *He's got strychnine poisoning; it may kill him.* I gave an injection that knocked him out, then left capsules with the family, saying, "Every time he rouses up, put a capsule in his rectum; don't let him wake up." And he survived.

Problem deliveries

One time I delivered a baby in a home down beyond Spring Creek, turning left just before you get to Law Road. The patient lived down in a hollow and was diabetic. The baby was already dead, and here I was trying to deliver it; when we weighed it later, I think it was 14 pounds. I worked and sweated; finally the head came out. Then I had to tie gauze around its neck and pull the rest of the body out by force. Thinking back on such incidents as these now, I wonder how I got through things like that without the facilities of a modern hospital.

Once a Mr. Johnson called me to attend his wife in childbirth. They lived out at Brown's Church. "Her water's leaking," he said. "Mr. Johnson," I asked, "is she having any labor pains? I hate to make that long a trip, with all these waiting to see me here in the office. If you'll wait until she starts having regular pains, let me know and I'll come." When he called again, I went over there, and waited and waited. Finally, after examining her, I said, "Mr. Johnson, the head is too big to engage in the birth canal. The baby is hydrocephalic; it has water on the brain." I explained that what I needed to do was carry her to the hospital, where I could go in under sterile conditions and do a craniotomy—puncture the skull and let the fluid out. Then the head could engage and the baby be delivered.

"No sir," he said, "I've had a one-armed doctor before, and he delivered my wife, and never had no trouble. You've been here several hours, and you mean to tell me that you can't deliver her?" "Well, then you get another doctor," I said. So he called old Dr. "X" in Jackson. I said, "Well, I won't leave; I'll wait here till he comes. I would hate to leave the patient by herself."

When Dr. X arrived, he examined her. I said, "Doctor, I really ought to carry her to the hospital, but they wouldn't let me." "Well, I'll see what *I* can do," he said. "Put her on the kitchen table." I yielded: "They called *you*. You're the doctor."

I tried giving the mother a little chloroform to keep her from suffering and from hollering so, while Dr. X went up in there, putting his forceps on the oversized head of the baby, only to have them slip off, again and again. He told me, "Give her a shot of pituitin." I said, "Doctor, I'm afraid to give her that, afraid it might rupture her uterus." "No, I don't think I've ever had any of 'em do that." "Well, if you order it, all right."

It seemed like this ordeal would never end. I don't know how many shots of pituitin I gave that poor woman, but finally I said, "Doctor, I've given her all I've got." But in the end, the baby's head did come out: huge, elongated, and deformed. By this time, of course, it was dead; I really don't remember if the baby's heart had stopped beating before Dr. X arrived. My recommendation, which would have allowed the baby to be born normally and might have saved its life, was totally ignored. The only other option would have been to do a Caesarean section, also in the hospital. But I would have been reluctant to do that after so much intrusion, for fear of infection.

But that's what happened in this case, and I never heard any more from the man or his wife. He paid the other doctor, but I never got a penny for all my trouble. To myself I said, *Before that happens again, I'll refuse to assist.*

Wrong turns

Heading home from the Johnsons before dawn the next morning, I took the wrong turn. Instead of coming out in Spring Creek, the next road sign I saw said "Chester Street." I thought perhaps I was in Lexington, but felt my way along until it hit me: *Here's Union University; I'm in Jackson!* So I took the long way home that morning.

One night I went out beyond Milan to see a new patient, following directions given me over the phone. I got there all right, but when I left the patient's home, driving on a blacktop road in the dark, I thought I had missed my turn. I doubled back to take the blacktop that seemed to be the right one. Well, I followed it until it came into town (which should have been Milan), and lo and behold, ahead of me I could see the peak of the Trenton courthouse!

Sleepless nights

Lillie May has reminded me of one night that I'd been out on a call and came home around 10:30 or 11:00 p.m. I was lying in bed reading (which I like to do to relax before going to sleep). Well, I got another call, had to get dressed and go out again, and got in at 2:30 or 3:00 a.m. Just about the time I had finally gotten off to a good sleep, around 4:30, Mr. Fate Graves called. He had given me a ticket to the Sunday School supper in Jackson, and couldn't wait to find out if I had enjoyed it!

Icy roads

Winters aren't severe in West Tennessee, but occasionally sleet or freezing rain will form ice on our roads. One night the roads were about as bad as they ever get here, an inch or so of ice covering everything. We had to use chains or spikes on our tires. Well, Mr. McLemore called me to come to Lavinia and see his wife. I said, "Mr. McLemore, I don't see how in the world I can get there; these roads are too bad." He kept begging, however, and so I went—only to find out that she really didn't need me. But returning on Spring Creek Road, as I was passing the home of Mr. Oma Nicholls near the Latham's Chapel turn-off, I guess one of my front wheels hit a brick or rock or clod of frozen dirt. My car spun 180°, so that it was heading in the opposite direction.

As I was maneuvering the car, trying to get back up that icy slope so I could turn around and go on home, Mr. Oma came out on his porch and yelled, "Who's out there?" I said, "It's Dr. Morris, trying to get my car turned around so I can get home. I never was in such a mess." Finally I got home, and had been in bed 45 minutes or more when Mr. Oma called and said, "Dr. Morris, we'd like for you to come out here." I said, "Mr. Oma, what happened? I just left your house!" "Well, Sarah Waller's over here visiting (that's their daughter), and she's having labor pains." "She wasn't supposed to have a baby for another month or six weeks." "Well, there's something wrong; we'd like for you to come."

So I got up, drove slowly over the icy road back to his house, and sure enough, I found Sarah in active labor. She gave birth to twins, a girl and a boy, weighing only about three-and-a-half pounds each. The girl was harelipped, with the hard palate open. The babies were so tiny that I thought, *They look like rats.* And since they arrived unexpectedly, the family had no clothes for them.

Mrs. Nicholls, though, was equal to the occasion. She was a very calm woman who let nothing disturb her. She began tearing sheets, folding some pieces into diapers and pinning others together into little shirts. I said, "Mrs. Nicholls, I don't know if you can raise these babies or not, but I reckon the only way we can feed this one"—the girl with the harelip—"is with a medicine dropper." Because she was unable to suckle, we fixed up a formula that could be fed to her with a dropper. Not long after her birth, I had the family take her to Nashville for the surgical repair of her harelip. Both babies survived: The boy graduated from Union University, and the girl married the Studdard boy who drives for UPS. She runs the post office in Spring Creek now; in fact, I delivered one of her children, which shows how my work really spanned two generations.

Danger stalking in the woods

One day a fellow came to me complaining of his rectum: He'd been out in the woods the day before, and had been hurting ever since. Examining his rectum, I found that he was bleeding a little, and felt something like a stick up in there. *What in the world?* I thought. So I had him lie on his side on the examining table, and stretched his rectum with a dilator. He hollered, and I said, "Be doggoned if I don't believe that's a blackberry stalk!" I took hold of it and gently moved it a little, with him squalling and hollering. I pulled out a two-inch piece of stalk with the briers still on it, and showed it to him, saying, "How in the world did you get this up in your rectum?! I can't see for my life, unless your rectum turned out, and then when it turned back in, it sucked in this piece of stalk."

Self-administered abortions

One time a woman called me to her home; she was bleeding from her womb. I asked her, "Have you done anything to yourself?" She finally confessed to me that yes, she had been trying to abort. She had poked a lollipop stick into the mouth of her womb, then squirted turpentine in with a medicine dropper. She had miscarried, and now had a high fever. I said, "Thank you. I'm glad you told me, because now I've got to fight an infection. And the question is, did [the placenta] all pass, or did anything get left in the womb?" She recovered from the infection, but ever after that, whenever I saw her, I'd think about this incident.

On another occasion, while performing an operation on a different patient, my colleague and I found a match, either in the woman's womb or in her ovarian tube. She had used that match trying to open the mouth of her womb to make herself miscarry.

Wife abuse

Once, while my office was still over the bank, I was suturing Mr. Luther Luckey's foot when the phone rang. This fellow said, "Please come quick as you can. I want you to see my wife." He lived down across the railroad track in one of the old section-hand houses. I went over there and found the wife prone on the front porch.

I said, "Well, let's pick her up and carry her inside. Wonder what in the world has happened that she should fall out?" We carried her in and put her on the bed. After talking to her a little bit, I observed that she was nervous and jittery. After taking her blood pressure and pulse, I gave her a capsule or two, saying, "This will help you get relaxed."

Meanwhile, I noticed their two little girls, maybe four to six years old, hiding behind the stove, all drawn up and shaking. The husband, however, was hovering over me, with his arm on the headboard. So I said, "Would you take this thermometer in the kitchen and wash it for me?" "All right," he said. As soon as he left the room, I put my mouth close to the woman's ear: "Did he hit you?" "Yes." "Thank you." I had found out what I wanted to know.

The man came back; he had busted my thermometer, putting it under hot water instead of cold. I said, "Mister, it's a shame that you would live this way in your home and do your wife this way. Look at those two little girls there, just scared to death." He replied, "Mister, I didn't ask you to tell me how to live; I called you to treat my wife." I said, "I don't find anything seriously wrong now. I've given her some medicine to quiet her. The medicine's in her stomach. I've done done *my* work; don't you *ever* call me again!" When, a month or two later, he came up on my porch and asked me to come again, I said, "What did I tell you, mister? I said I won't go." And I didn't.

But I learned something from that incident: to be careful when I told another fellow how he ought to live, unless I had solid grounds for admonishing him.

One foot in the grave

Old Mrs. Kirk had been left a widow at a young age, with two little boys, and she never remarried. Her son delivered papers. Mrs. Kirk might be seen coming down the railroad track, carrying a woven splitwood basket full of eggs and butter.

She took sick when she was perhaps 92, and got in a stuporous state. She wouldn't eat, wouldn't answer questions, and her blood pressure was gradually failing. After she had been in this state a week or more, her son asked me one night, as I completed my examination of her,

"Doctor, how long do you think Mother will live?" I said, "Mr. Kirk, I doubt she'll live another 48 hours; maybe she'll be living tomorrow."

At this point old Mrs. Kirk raised up and said, "Why, I will live to eat the goose that eats the grass that grows on your grave!"

"Mr. Kirk, would you believe that?" I said. "If I hadn't been here and heard it for myself, I wouldn't have believed it." And apparently she never said another word before she died the next day.

Mrs. & Mrs. B. B. Kirk in 1947. This does not appear to be the "old Mrs. Kirk" of the "One foot in the grave" incident, but it illustrates the style of clothing worn through the 1940s and a woven splitwood basket that might be used for carrying eggs.

CHAPTER XVII

HOBBIES AND LEISURE

Medical meetings

When I first came to Medina, our county medical meetings were held in Trenton. Dr. Weldon Oliver and I would ride together, and if the weather was cold we would lay a buggy lapspread over our legs. Later, the county medical meetings were replaced by the Consolidated Medical Association, which drew from a 12-county area, with meetings being held in Jackson, as they are today.[1] I began attending these meetings, which were first held in the old Jackson jail and, later, upstairs in the Southern Hotel. I attended these meetings faithfully until four or five years ago; I guess I had the best attendance record in the organization until I began cutting back on my practice. Also, in the early 1950s, perhaps 1954, I was elected president for one year.

As president, I had the responsibility of moderating business meetings and of securing and introducing guest speakers. Two of my speakers were DeCosta, the author of a textbook on surgery, and Harwell Wilson, a Memphis surgeon and, at that time, president of the Tennessee Medical Association.

Too, I participated in the West Tennessee Medical Association whenever it had programs of interest, and a few times I went to the state medical association meetings in Nashville.[2]

The big Mid-South medical meetings were held in Memphis and, when I attended, I usually stayed overnight in the home of Dr. Tom West. He was a good friend, with a guest wing on his house. I'd eat breakfast with Tom, his wife, and their four children. On my forty-fifth birthday, Tom came to Medina and brought me a handsome leather medical bag as a present.

Portrait of Dr. Morris that hangs in Jackson General Hospital, where he was a consulting staff physician. Probably taken in 1989.

During the past several years, until the present (1989), I have been regularly attending Tuesday "ward rounds" at the Jackson-Madison County General Hospital. These gatherings consist of a luncheon followed by some presentation. Typical subjects are new drugs and unusual cases.

Reading his Bible—a daily habit of Dr. Morris throughout adult life; here in 1988. Photo by LLM.

Church involvement

As a teenager, following baptism, I joined the Gibson Baptist Church, and remained a member there until I went to medical school. When I resided in Memphis, I was an active member of Bellevue Baptist Church, pastored by Dr. R. G. Lee. He began there only shortly before I arrived, and remained throughout my six years in Memphis. After completing my internship, I moved my membership back to Gibson. Then in 1937, within a week or two after we came to Medina, I moved my membership to First Baptist Church here, where it has remained ever since.

A year or two after my arrival in Medina, I was asked to teach the young men's Sunday School class—men in their twenties and thirties. And ever since then, except for time out when I was sick and when I lived with my daughter Lillie, I have taught a men's Bible class. My class, the Seekers, now has men in their 60s and early 70s. Bobby Don Harris has taken over the class at my request when I have been unable to teach.[3] In 1940, church officers approached me about being a deacon. We discussed the responsibilities involved, and I agreed to accept nomination. The church elected me as deacon on November 8, 1940, and I have continued to serve in this capacity ever since.

I surround myself with Bibles and sermons. I mostly watch religious programs on TV. I also like to be with Christian people. That's why, whenever they have a special program at Union University—a preaching series or a revival—I will attend. My favorite is the annual Preachers' School, a weeklong session every summer. There are two services in the morning, two in the afternoon, and two at night. They bring in the leading preachers in the Southern Baptist Convention. I have attended this for years.

Baseball

While medical practice and church involvement took up most of my time, I have always enjoyed sports, and for several years played baseball in Medina. At one time we used a field near the brick kiln beyond Oakfield.

But one night we were playing baseball in the schoolyard behind my house, and I ran back between the parked cars to catch a fly ball. I slipped and fell on the dewy grass, hurting my tailbone and my heel. Hoping my heel was merely sprained, I went on and played out the game, but kept thinking: *I declare, this is a terrible pain for a sprain!*

That night, when I got home, I went to bed, and my heel was hurting quite a bit. Then someone knocked outside, and I tried to get out of bed to answer the door. My goodness! When I put my foot down, I fell in the floor, the pain was so severe; I had to crawl to the door. And so, the next day, I went to the hospital and had my foot X-rayed.[4] The X-ray showed that I had a fracture through the heelbone, and, as a result, I had to wear a walking cast for six weeks. Being past 40, I reasoned with myself: *At my age, I'd better quit playing ball.*

Basketball

Although I never got interested in playing golf or games like that, I did enjoy going to the basketball games over here at the high school as long as my daughters Trebor and Brenda were playing. And sometimes I would go see them play in Milan or Humboldt. Outside of that, I never went much. I had enjoyed basketball as a boy, however, as I mentioned in the chapter on "Growing Up."

Football

Almost every year, I would get to a few football games. Sometimes I'd go down to Oxford, Mississippi, to see Ole Miss play a Tennessee school. And I usually saw one post-season game. Twice I went to New Orleans to the Sugar Bowl: Quentin Murphree and I went to Gulfport or Biloxi and got a motel room, then the next morning drove up the coast to New Orleans to see the game. When it was over, we doubled back on old Highway 45 to Medina. Also, twice I went with Quentin to the Cotton Bowl in Dallas.

Left: Father and son in backyard, in period 1946–48. Dr. Morris loved sports, and kept this picture by his bedside until he died. Robert was not athletic, but Trebor and Brenda played main-string basketball in high school. *Right:* In his garden, 1954. Dr. Morris last farmed when he was 26 years old, but working in his garden was a relaxing hobby for the rest of his life.

One time I also went to the 'Gator Bowl in Jacksonville, Florida, when Tennessee and Texas played. Trebor and Melton went with George Parrish and myself, but whereas George and I already had our tickets, Melton and Trebor were unable to buy theirs and so missed the game.

Too, once or twice I went with Walter Hunt to Knoxville when Alabama played Tennessee. Then when Tennessee would play a big game in Memphis, I would make it if I could. But my practice was such that I couldn't get off frequently to attend games.

Good next-door neighbors and friendly gardening rivals, Dr. Morris and Abe Utley (both raised on farms) here relax and chat—facing their gardens, of course. Photo 1986 by LLM.

Television viewing

My regular programs are news, the 700 Club, and Bible teachers. I also watch sports—mostly basketball and football, post-season bowl games especially. I try to have my Sunday School lesson prepared before Sunday morning, so I can watch religious programs before church. My wife will want to see "What Is Your Faith?" then I will turn back to Channel 12 and get Dr. D. James Kennedy and Dr. DeHaan.

Gardening

I always managed to grow a home vegetable garden. *RMII: Dad grew a sizable garden in our back yard every year until 1989, when he only set out a few plants; in 1990 he made no attempt. For many years, this garden provided a good portion of our table food. Usually a local farmer would break the ground in the spring with his tractor, but I have also seen Dad borrow a mule and break it himself. In his last years of gardening, he used a Troy-bilt rototiller.*

Dad and Abe Utley next door carried on a friendly rivalry in their gardens for years, which was appropriate since both had been farmers up into their adult years.

Often Dad would get out in the garden early in the morning before breakfast; perhaps he would scratch a few rows at noon; and he would work it again in the late afternoon. I believe it was relaxing for him, as well as economically productive. He often got me to help him, and taught me how to do it the "right" way.

CHAPTER XVIII

THE COMING OF MODERN CONVENIENCES

Of horses and cars

The automobile was not yet available to the public when I was born in 1904, and, except for the train that ran through Gibson, horses and mules provided the only means of transportation in our community. We rode them and used them to pull buggies, surreys, and wagons. At our church, off to the north side of the building, a cable strung on posts served to hitch the horses and mules. But for any distance up to a mile, such as going to church or school, my family usually walked.

Half of the pupils walked to the Gibson school from their homes in the morning and back again in the afternoon, some from as far away as three miles; they thought nothing of it. Generally, those living farther away would be brought in wagons; a man might bring a wagonload from his community. In rainy weather, everyone would have umbrellas and raincoats as they rode in the open wagons. A few parents would bring and pick up their children in surreys or buggies. A small number of the older children rode horses to school; some were stabled in a barn on the lot where Dr. Hunt's first house stood. Virgie Morse[1] drove her own buggy, and John White's children, William and Mary,[2] drove a buggy that was stored in our barn. Walker "Squirrel" Langford kept his horse down the street from the school in the barn of his grandfather, John Langford.

My family never owned a tractor when I was growing up, and I have never driven one. All our farm machinery—plow, harrow, hay mower, and rake—was horse-drawn. We had seven or eight head of horses and mules. Sometimes Dr. Hunt would be paid for his medical services with a calf, colt, or young mule. I rode horseback a lot. As a little boy, I liked to ride behind Grandpa on his doctor calls. Or, when he would come in from a call, he would put me on the horse, telling me to ride him down to the pond and let him drink.

I remember that one time Grandpa brought home a new horse and told me, "Carry him on down there and let him drink." I rode him to the pond, and when we got to the water, all of a sudden he just flopped over in the pond to wallow. I jumped off and thought he was drowning, so I screamed and hollered, "Come quick! This horse is gonna drown!" Later I found out that this horse had the habit of wallowing, but it was something I had never seen a horse do.

Sometimes I had to go to the far pasture to drive our cow (or cows) in, so I would get on the horse. It was a mile or more over there and as much back—down beyond the barn, then across a big ditch and back up through the woods to the corner of the farm. Because bitterweed would ruin the taste of the milk, I might have to take the cow and stake her out where no bitterweed was growing.

Cars come to Gibson

Then Uncle Charlie, Papa's brother who lived in Batesville, Mississippi, bought a car and drove it up to visit us. I had heard about cars, of course, but never thought much about them because no one in Gibson had a car and I had never seen one. So this was the first car I ever saw; to me it looked like a wagon. It had a chain drive—a chain on each side that turned the back wheels.

After this, it was a long time before I saw another car. When they did arrive in Gibson, they were usable only in dry weather, because we had dirt roads. Jerry Brewer became the first person in our town to own a car; he bought a little Hupmobile. It had one or two bulbs on it to honk; also you had to crank it, and it would just spit and pop. Everybody said, "Jerry Brewer is going to get killed. It'll blow up!" Often it would stop, and he'd have to get out and crank and crank.

Then Mr. Brewer began selling cars. He brought a brass-radiator Ford up to Dr. Hunt's house, and finally persuaded my grandfather to buy it. It had a top like a buggy, curtains to close it in, and a little bulb on the side that you'd push—*Oogah, oogah!* Under the steering wheel were two levers —one for the spark plug and one for the gas feed; then three foot pedals— the clutch on the left, reverse in the middle, and the brake on the right.

Dr. Hunt's horseless carriage adventures

Now, Grandpa Hunt had either ridden a horse or driven a buggy or surrey all his life. By this time, he was over 60 years old, and a lot of people said, "He'll never learn to drive one of those things." Well, as you will see, there was some truth to that, but he was brave enough to try it, although he had a stiff arm.

One day, when Grandpa was on his way home after a call, he was passing Mr. Manley's tomato field when he lost control somehow. The car jumped the little ditch, plowed into that tomato field, and he drove on down the row—I don't know how far. People laughed about that for a long time. Then one day we were out in the country, and he started to back up, but there was a post behind the car; he hit it, tried again, and hit it again. This happened over and over, so I said, "Grandpa, better stop the thing! We're not getting anywhere like this." Finally he stopped, saying, "Well, I'd better just drive on, and not try to turn around."

At that time Grandpa's entire front lawn was fenced in, with a gate and with an inner fence surrounding the house. He let animals graze on the front lawn—a calf or two, then sometimes (that is, back before he got a car) Grandpa would turn his horse loose to cool off in the shade and graze when he came in from a call; peacocks and guinea hens were out there, too. After Grandpa got his Ford, whenever I was around his house I would open the gate for him so he could drive out, then close it behind him. I'd say, "Grandpa, let me just ride to the gate, and I'll open it for you." But one time, while we were driving toward the gate, I somehow kicked his medicine case over. Well, he just turned the steering wheel loose, reached down to pick up the medicine case, and *wham!*—we hit a tree. The steering rods were bent into a **V** under the car, which caused the wheels to collapse under the motor. "Well, I've done it now!" Grandpa said. "Go catch the horse and hitch up my buggy for me."

But I would do anything just to ride a short distance in that brass-radiator Ford. One time Papa sent me up on the hill to plow a five-acre field, but I knew the family was going over to Medina that afternoon. So I plowed without a break, not even for lunch, finishing before two o'clock so I could ride in that car with them. And every time we would meet a buggy on that dusty road, the horses (they weren't used to automobiles yet) would start rearing and lunging. So we'd have to kill the motor, stop and let the horses go by, then get out and crank the motor again. They'd say, "Watch out! watch out! Don't give it too much spark plug! If it doesn't catch, it'll kick you, and you might break your arm!"

Dr. Hunt kept his brass-radiator Ford in a garage that he had built out beside his house, placing the garage on a concrete foundation. Now, having dealt all his life with horses who understood spoken commands, he naturally tried the same approach with horseless carriages. We would laugh as we watched him driving into his garage, hollering 'Whoa! whoa! whoa!', and not stopping until he hit the back wall. Over a period of time he pounded that wall so much that he shifted the garage off its foundation, and it had to be set back in place.

Getting in a rut

The use of automobiles continued to grow until the dirt road in front of our house was deep with dust from cars running back and forth. Paul Sires, for one, would drive down the street at 35 or 40 miles per hour, the dust just rolling onto the lawns and gardens on both sides. You could write your name on our front porch because of the dust on it. Then, when it rained—*mud*. Your car had to be equipped with high-pressure tires to go through the mud. You'd chug along, chug along, and sooner or later get into a rut, and you'd have to stay in that rut. The only trouble then was that, when you met a car coming in the opposite direction, one of you had to get out of the rut. Sometimes you could back up and cut a groove in the side of the rut, then pull off and let the other fellow get by; but if you didn't watch out, you'd slip off into the ditch.

Close scrapes

I've never been seriously hurt in an automobile, but I've had a couple of close calls. In one incident during World War II, after the Milan Arsenal had been opened, doctors were invited to come up for a dinner and for a tour of the plant. So I rode over with several others from our medical society, including Henry and Stanford Herron. We were riding around the "Area," as we called it, getting a general tour, and going 35 miles per hour over blacktop roads, when a member of our party said, "I believe one of our tires is going down, the way it's knocking." "Well, I'll roll the window down and look," I said. But when I leaned against the door, it wasn't latched—just held by a screen-door spring—and of course it flew open. I was thrown out, and went rolling down the blacktop. I lost my thermometer, my pens, my prescription blanks—everything that was in my vest pockets. The others were saying, "Listen, I bet we killed him!" And brother, that shook me up; I was so nauseous I couldn't enjoy my supper with them after that tour. But I wasn't seriously hurt.

Then once Lillie May persuaded me to go with her and five other women to Camden, Tennessee, to see Mr. and Mrs. Don Smith, former residents of Medina. Mrs. Elam was driving her three-seated van. I was sitting in the front seat on the passenger side. We were on the concrete highway approaching Camden, with gravel trucks coming by us pretty fast heading the other way. Mrs. Elam decided to pass the little truck ahead of us, but just as she was pulling into the left lane, a car that she hadn't seen whizzed by us in the opposite direction. She jerked the wheel to pull back into our lane, over-corrected, and we began weaving. Our van flopped over on its side and scooted along the pavement. Looking down through the window at the concrete rushing under me, I thought, *This is it!* But we skidded across the highway; the front wheel engaged in the shoulder of the roadway, and the van stood up on its front end for a moment, then dropped over on its top, heading in the opposite direction.

When we first flipped over, my side must have hit the window crank on the door, because it was hurting. Unable to get my door open, I crawled over the back of the front seat to where most of the women were, with their food dishes dumped all over them and the van. Finally

I cranked down the back door window and wriggled out. Gasoline was leaking, and I said to the ladies, "You'd better get out of there if you can; this thing might catch on fire!"

My side was hurting pretty bad, but all of them got out. So, while we were sitting on the bank waiting for help to come, some fellow stopped and said, "My goodness alive! How many were killed in that?" I said, "Our seven have come out of it. I don't know whether there are any left in there or not. But it's a wonder we *haven't* been killed."

So we had to call Reau Graves and have him come up from Medina and get the old van. If we hadn't been fortunate, we could have turned over in the big ditch just beyond the point where we went off the road. It was filled with water, and quite possibly we would have drowned.

I was x-rayed two or three times, but they never found a broken bone. However, it was about six weeks before the pain in my side subsided. I guess that's the nearest I've come to being killed in an automobile; so far, I haven't had a serious accident when I was the driver.

(RMII: Dad did have a minor accident in early 1990. Coming over a hill, he ran into the back of a pickup truck. He cut his head, and this contributed to the decline of his health through the final year of his life.)

OTHER INVENTIONS

Radio and television

Back in the early Twenties, I was helping my father apply canvas to the walls at the home of Mr. Phil Jones, in preparation for papering. Mr. Jones was the railroad depot agent in Gibson, and he owned a farm near the cemetery. He had scientific curiosity and would study any new thing that came out. After learning about radios, he had made himself a little one. Well, Papa and I had never seen or heard one; we had just heard *about* them. So while we were working in his house, Mr. Jones brought this contraption in and said, "Put these earplugs in your ears"—and we heard music playing. I said, "Where is this coming from?" He said 'Chicago,' or some other place out-of-state, and added, "You know what? There's not a wire between us and there!" "You don't *mean* it?! You mean, coming from Illinois or Kentucky, and not a wire between us?!" We were used to telephones by that time, but we thought this wireless invention was a marvel.

Others in Medina got televisions before I did. I used to watch ball games with Paul Gowan on his TV. I waited until the mid-1950s to get one, because I knew it might keep my kids from studying. I kept my first set, a Zenith, 15 years, then gave it to Brenda after receiving the color television they gave me at the Morris Appreciation Day. That set was good up to the 1980s, then I bought the RCA that I used until late 1989, when my son-in- law Melton Ambrose gave me a new set in exchange for my Troy-bilt rototiller.

Electricity

During most of my school years in Gibson, we used coal-oil lamps. These had glass bowls, wicks, and chimneys. At home, we'd have to put one right on the table to study, or right by the sewing machine to use it. Later, when the Aladdin lamp came out, which had a circular wick and a pump (to create fuel pressure), it gave off a very brilliant white light, similar to the camping lamps used today, and we thought it was a marvel.

I don't know what year electricity came to Gibson, but when our home was first wired, we had lines installed in only two or three rooms. We were afraid to do more, because we thought it would cost too much. Each room where we put a light had two little wires coming down from the center of the ceiling, with a light socket and a pull chain attached.

When the lights were first installed and my daddy turned one on, I said, "Isn't that *something*, whew! We've got light now; we can throw the old lamps away!" But Daddy warned me, "Sonny, listen: When you go out of this door, you turn that light off! Because it's going to cost us at least $2.50 a month to pay for it, and we can't afford it." He so trained me that, to this day, anytime I come in a room and see a light on without somebody in there, I think, *How foolish!. Why in the world is the light burning in here?* And when I walk through the house, I turn them off.

CHAPTER XIX

OBSERVATIONS ON MYSELF

Now I see myself

Basically, I am not the kind of person I have wanted to be. Looking back over my life, it makes me miserable to think about the things I've done that I shouldn't have. But one principle has stuck with me all my life: I have tried to please my parents. I wanted my father's commendation for doing what he had said. As a boy, if he assigned me a task, saying, "You ought to plow that field today," I looked forward to getting the field plowed that day. When I got home he'd ask, "Did you finish it?" "Yes, sir, I got it done." "Well, you had to work to do it!" Or perhaps: "Did you get those tomatoes plowed today?" "Yes, sir." "You did exactly what I said to do." I wanted him to know that I had worked when he wasn't watching me and had measured up to his expectations.

I remember carrying a plow over to Grandpa Morris's place in order to work his bottomland for him. Papa told me, "You ought to get that bottom plowed today," and he showed me how to get the plow in the wagon: "Put the beam of the plow in first; bring it around; put it on the end of the bed; take the handles, come around, and you can get this plow on the wagon." I looked forward to breaking that ground before the day ended, and when I got home I said, "Well, I got it done!" Something about getting the job done was stamped in me.

Also, I guess I've been somewhat of a perfectionist—I want to do something exactly like it should be done. And if I or someone else fails to do it that way, it worries me: *That isn't the way it should be done! He ought not to have done it that way!* I was this way about my medical practice. If something I did or a medicine I prescribed got bad results, or if the patient had trouble, I worried: *What in the world did I do wrong?* It bothered me to be wrong on a diagnosis.

I am time-conscious as well. *Today I need to get so-and-so done, and I have this much time to do it in.* Every day I get up thinking, *I've got this to do today*—cut the yard, or whatever. And as quick as I can, I'll get that done.

I guess that, by nature, I am an introvert; I don't shove out and take the lead; I'm reserved. However, I do feel more comfortable in small groups. Since 1938 I have taught Sunday School, and since 1940 have served as church deacon. My Sunday School class at one time had 30 members— John Morgan, Charlie Cash, Roy Graves, Raymond Davidson, and the other men. Then, too, one year I was president of our local medical association and had to introduce the speakers as well as chair the business meetings. More recently, I've made impromptu speeches on occasions when I've been publicly honored, but then I was speaking about myself, which is quite different from delivering a prepared speech on some topic.

Money

I was always concerned that I might have overcharged someone, but then I'd think back: *Well, that's all you're charging; how COULD you have overcharged him?* But the Bible has impressed on me not to be an extortioner, and I want to do what is right. Dr. Leland Johnson in Jackson used to tell me, "Bob, how are you going to make a living, with five children, charging $2, $2.50, and $3 a call, and $25 to deliver a baby?! I don't see how it can be done!" And in fact, throughout most of my years of practice, that's what I charged. I did get $5 for some home calls, and finally began charging $7 if I went to Law, Spring Creek, and other places farther out. But up to that time I used to go for $5, even $3, all over this country— including Lavinia, Oakfield, and Christmasville Road. Still, in spite of my modest fees, a few patients would grumble that I was charging too much.

A certain doctor in Milan used to tell me how much land and how many houses he owned, and I'd say to myself, *Lord golly! I've just barely got a home and a living!* And when our children were in college (three of them at the same time, one year), checks would come in to the bank that my balance wouldn't cover. Ray Rowlett would call and say, "Dr. Morris, there's a check come in here. Can you make it up?" I said, "Ray, I haven't got the money right now. But I'll tell you one thing: As quick as I can get it, I'll be down there and pay you." Bankers won't do this today, but he would hold the check for one, two, or maybe three days, and when I collected some money I'd go straight to him to pay it.

I remember one time when the financial pressure was weighing on me, driving around a curve on the Spring Creek Road, talking to myself: *"Life does not consist in the abundance of things which you have."*[1] *. . . Well, at least I'm making a living, and finally have my home paid out!*

While my income was above the average for Medina, the druggist and some of those in plumbing, banking, business, and insurance were making more than I was. Patients would come back to me after buying drugs I had prescribed, complaining about the cost. (This was true especially when the mycetin drugs and penicillin came out, a dose costing $5 to $7, or a prescription for 15 or 20 capsules costing $15 to $20.) They'd say, "What in the world did you give me?" "I was giving you this new drug. I don't control the price; it's the druggist." "Don't you get part of it?" "No, there's not a thing sold in that drugstore that I get any percent." And in spite of what some people thought, I never had a share in the drugstore nor a deal with the druggist.

I did briefly own a share in the Doctors' Hospital in Jackson, along with Drs. Johnson, Chandler, Myhr, and Wylie. I had either $3,000 or $5,000 invested in it when it opened, but after two or three months, I told Leland Johnson and the others, "Being the distance I am from Jackson, and my practice being like it is, I don't think I have the means to invest. I need the money and would like to withdraw." So they gave me my money back, and outside of that little venture, I just earned my living from my local practice.[2]

My strengths and weaknesses

The biggest obstacle to achieving according to my ability has been an inferiority complex, the feeling that "I can't do it; I can't accomplish it; I don't have the strength to do it." In reality, I have tended to depreciate my ability. For instance, in medical school I was actually making the grades; still I felt like I couldn't do the work and that I'd never finish.

The strengths in my character come from my religious faith and training. My daddy pounded in me all the time: "In all your ways acknowledge Him, and He will direct your paths"[3]—in other words, put God first. I saw, in my parents and grandparents, independence and a determination to go on regardless of circumstances, to trust in the Lord that things would work out some way. Looking back over my life, I never would have succeeded without the Lord's help. Although I didn't realize it at times like I should have, now I can see that His hand has been at work in my life throughout.

I was taught to be honest and to tell the truth. Although I took some coins when I was little, the Lord convicted me of that so strongly that ever since then I don't remember deliberately taking or stealing from anybody; I don't want to. I believe in talking straight, too. I'd tell my patients, "I hate to tell you, but *this* is what you've got."

I've tried to live at peace with my neighbors. I'd rather overlook a wrong done to me if I can. When I was having a fence put up along one side of our back yard, my neighbor moved the stake a foot or so in from our property line. I noticed this and told my wife, who started to get heated up about it. But I told Mr. Moore, who was stringing the fence for me, to leave the stake there. I said, "What is a little old fence? If it *is* a foot, let him have it!"

When we were having the Little House built out back, we set it close to our property line. This same neighbor complained, "The water will fall on my side, the way you are building it." So I told the builder to cut the rafters off a foot shorter than planned. I said, "Just cut them off and let the water fall down on my side."

My relationship with God

I've never had complete peace or satisfaction in my religious experience. I read in the Bible about a "peace that passes understanding,"[4] and I've said, "Well, Lord, it doesn't look like I've ever attained peace to that extent." As I reflect on my conversion, the question still haunts me, *Did you get all you can get?* All I can do is go back to that time and remember what happened; I still have not attained what I have wanted. I've begged the Lord, "Give me more. I want more faith. I want to please Thee." I see where I've failed Him so miserably.

But I do have the assurance of the Spirit and the promises of Scripture that I am a child of God, and if I didn't have that I would die or go crazy. My main interest in life is watching religious programs on TV and reading religious literature. I have piles of books all around me by Chuck Colson, D. James Kennedy, Billy Graham, and others like them.

CHAPTER XX

OUR CHILDREN, GRANDCHILDREN, AND GREAT-GRANDCHILDREN[1]

Una Deane

Una entered the University of Tennessee, Martin Branch (now officially the "University of Tennessee-Martin") in the fall of 1954. She obtained her B.A. degree in 1957 with a major in home economics. (In 1979 she also obtained her M.A. equivalency from the state of Tennessee.)

While at UT-Martin, Una met William Craig Grant from Alamo, Tennessee, a pre-med student. Craig had served in the U.S. Navy during the Korean War. Upon completing his bachelor degree, he entered the University of Tennessee Medical School in Memphis. Una moved to Memphis also, and entered cytology (cancer research) training with UT medical units. (Incidentally, hers was the first class to admit blacks.) Then, from 1958 to 1962, she served as a therapeutic dietitian at John Gaston Hospital, now called "The Med."

Craig married Una during his fifth quarter of medical school, and graduated first in his class. He was a general surgery resident for two years, and later completed a neurosurgery residency under Semmes and Murphy at Baptist Memorial Hospital in Memphis. For one year, he practiced with Case Gottlieb in Yakima, Washington; then he brought his family back to Memphis, where he practiced with the Memphis Neurosurgical Group until his death in 1987.

Five children were born to Craig and Una: Cherie (1959), William ("Bill" or "Bubba," 1960), James Andrew ("Andy," 1962), Catheryne (1967), and Robert Browning ("Robb" or "Brownie," 1970). In 1975, after 17 years of marriage, Craig left Una, and they were divorced in 1977, leaving the children in her custody. Since then, Una has remained in Memphis to raise and assist her children. Craig remarried, but died suddenly in January, 1987, while vacationing in Florida.

Left: William Craig Grant, M.D., in 1974. *Center:* Cherie and Bill Morgan with their first child, Brittany *(foreground);* behind them stand, *l. to r.,* Catheryne, Robert Browning, William, and Andrew. Taken 1983. *Right:* Una Deane Grant with Brittany, also 1983.

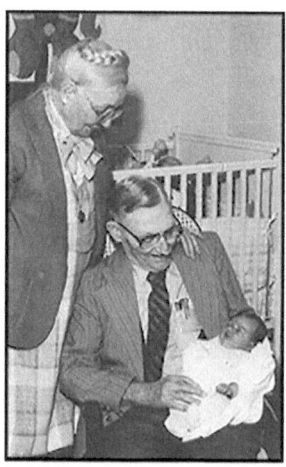

"Mamaw" and "Papaw" with first great-grandson, William Brandon Grant Morgan, born February 15, 1984; here one week old..

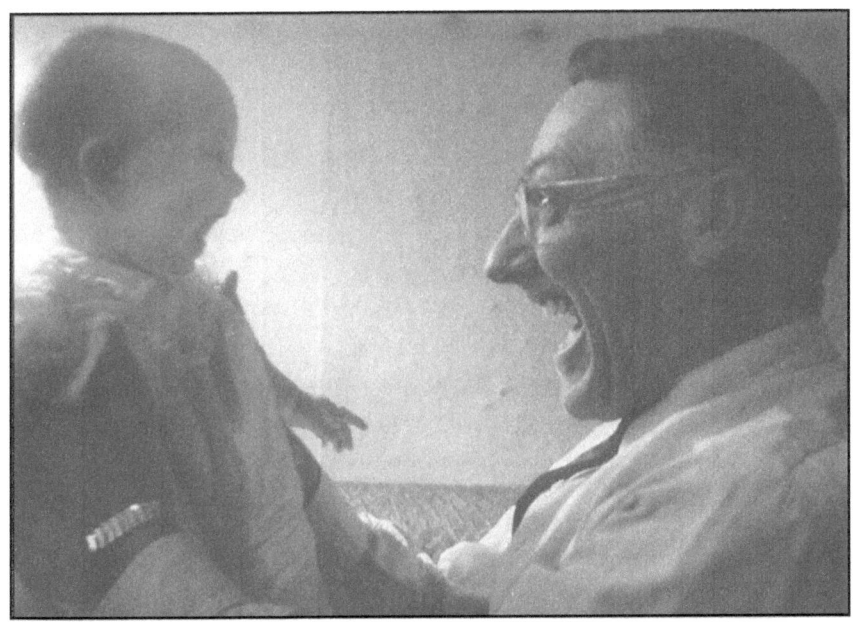

Dr. Morris enjoys his first grandchild, Cherie Anise Grant, in 1959.

As of spring 1990, Una is still living in Memphis on Carnes Avenue, near the campus of Memphis State University. She volunteers as a crisis counselor for women, and is working to market designs and ideas she has developed over the past 10 years.

Cherie studied art, then in 1978 married William "Bill" Morgan of Memphis, and today they have two children, Brittany (b. 1983) and Grant (b. 1984). Bill is employed both with Great Dane Trailers and with Federal Express Corporation.

William Grant married Vicki Petty in 1986. Vicki had graduated from Memphis State University in 1985 with a B.B.A. degree. Their current home is in Virginia Beach, Virginia, where William is based while serving in the U.S. Navy. Bill is a petty officer, working in damage control aboard the U.S.S. *Whidbey Island.* Vicki is a certified paralegal assistant, currently at home with their two daughters, Carrie (b. 1986) and Katelyn (b. 1989). *(UPDATE 1991: William's vessel was on stand-by duty in the Mediterranean during the Persian Gulf War.)*

Andrew resides in Memphis. He attended the State Technical Institute of Memphis in 1986, and is a musician and craftsman. He plays with the Mama Terra band.

Catheryne graduated in 1989 with a B.A. degree from Millsaps College in Mississippi, where she majored in English literature and minored in business. She is currently (1990) a certified leasing and sales specialist for C.L.A.S.S. Corporation, based in Atlanta, Georgia.

Robert Browning is completing his second year (spring 1990) at the University of Tennessee in Knoxville and is majoring in business administration. *(UPDATE 1991: Brownie completed his junior year at UT-Knoxville, and in summer 1991 began a co-op program with the International Paper Company in Memphis.*

Melton Crosby Ambrose, M.D. and Trebor Morton Ambrose, surrounded by their four sons *(left to right):* Richie Alan, Mel Jr., Mike, and John Robert. Photo taken in 1978.

Trebor

Trebor graduated from Medina High School as valedictorian in 1956, and after one full year at UT-Martin transferred to Union University in Jackson, where in 1959 she completed her

B.S., majoring in math and biology. Her fiancé, Melton Ambrose from Humboldt, attended Southwestern at Memphis (now Rhodes College) for one year, then, like Trebor, transferred to Union. They married in 1958 while both were still in school.

Melton entered UT Medical School in Memphis, obtaining his M.D. in 1962. He served in the Army for two years, as a physician with the rank of captain. Then he received further training in ophthalmology, having periods of residency in Boston and Houston. Melton and Trebor settled in Florence, Alabama, and remain there today. Melton is in group practice. Their home is both large and lovely.

Trebor and Melton have four sons: Mel (b. 1961). Mike (b. 1963), Richie (b. 1969), and John Robert (b. 1976). Mel and Mike both graduated from Auburn University, and Richie is now (spring 1990) completing his third year there. John, now completing the seventh grade, attends Mars Hill, a private academy near Florence. *(UPDATE 1991: Mike is back in school [University of Alabama in Huntsville], in chemical engineering.)*

Mel II received a B.S. in chemical engineering in 1985, and married Cyndy Longshore that same year. They lived for several years in Richmond, Virginia, where Mel worked for Allied Chemical, then they moved back to Florence, where he is currently employed with the T.V.A. Mel's hobby is woodworking; he also is devoted to teaching in the Church of Christ. Mel and Cyndy have one son, "Little Mel" (Melton III), born 1988, and their second child is due in the fall of 1991. (*UPDATE*: Stephen Longshore Ambrose arrived 8/27/91.)

Brenda

Like Trebor, Brenda graduated from Medina High (1958) at the head of her class. She spent two years at Freed-Hardeman College in Henderson, Tennessee, where she obtained an associate degree and met her husband-to-be, Ed Nulter, from Vienna, West Virginia.

For two years, Brenda pursued a certificate in medical technology, training while working at Jackson-Madison County General Hospital. But, after passing the national board exam, she decided to return to college, this time to UT-Martin. She majored in science education and graduated in 1964 with a B.S. degree. Shortly afterward, she and Ed were married. Ed's last two college years were at Bethel in McKenzie, Tennessee, and by the time of their marriage he had received teacher's training in Henry, Tennessee, and had taught public school two years in Missouri.

Harry Edwin and Brenda Leake Nulter with their children *(left to right):* Jill, Kelley, and Bryant. Photo taken Dec. 1982.

Myrtle McCrea of Milan had a sister, Mary Harris Code, in Huntsville, Alabama, and suggested to Ed and Brenda that it was a good place to teach. After investigating, they both applied for jobs in Huntsville, then moved there, and there they remain today. They have three children: Jill (b. 1967), Bryant "Bear" (b. 1968), and Kelley (b. 1971).

After Jill was born, Brenda stayed home nine-and-a-half years until all the children were in school, then she returned to teaching. Both Ed and Brenda now have masters' degrees in secondary education from the University of Alabama in Tuscaloosa. Brenda's major was science; Ed's was physical education. Today Ed coaches in junior high, while Brenda teaches high school chemistry. Hopefully they can retire in seven years.

Jill married Jeff Meier of Nashville, Tennessee, in 1988. They have a daughter, Excene Vawn, and a son, Kurt Louis. The Meiers have moved to Huntsville, where both Jill and Jeff are enrolled at the University of Alabama. Jeff is working towards a degree in engineering, and Jill is in a pre-dentistry program.

Bryant briefly attended Calhoun Junior College and UA-Huntsville, and for one year attended Mississippi State University in Starkville. He worked a year for Boeing, and now has plans to return to college in engineering.

Kelley graduated from high school in June, 1990, and attends the University of Montevallo near Birmingham, Alabama, where she is doing well.

Robert Hunt

In 1959, Robert became our third child to graduate as a Medina High School valedictorian. He obtained his B.A. degree in 1963 from Southwestern at Memphis (now Rhodes College), majoring in French and spending his junior year in Aix-en-Provence, France. Entering Princeton University in the fall of 1963 on a full humanities fellowship, he left after one semester, and in the years since then has done various types of work: jobs requiring office/secretarial skills; street work and paraprofessional social work (in New York); cabinetmaking (New York and North Carolina); and teaching in a Christian school. More recently, in Texas, he has served as associate editor of the Center for Judaic-Christian Studies, a Bible research organization; and, since 1986, as a proofreader and typesetter with G&S Typesetters, Inc., working on textbooks and university press publications. Robert's hobby is writing, and he has developed and taught several adult Bible courses. *(UPDATE 1991: Robert has taken one course in Hebrew at the University of Texas-Austin, and in August 1991 plans to move to Tulsa, Oklahoma, where he will enter a graduate program in Biblical studies at Oral Roberts University. His goal is to do original research, writing, and teaching at the college level.)*

Robert married Jeanne Elizabeth Sokol of Unadilla, New York, in 1968. Prior to marriage, Jeanne had obtained her B.A. degree from the State University of New York at Oneonta and had completed her practice teaching. Following their wedding, Jeanne worked with children in various New York City settings until their first child was born in 1973, after which she stayed at home until all their children were in school. In 1985, she returned to part-time work, first in a Christian bookstore, but more recently providing in-home services for the elderly. *(UPDATE 1991: In November 1990, Jeanne completed a two-month training program and passed the state exam to become a certified Nurse Aide; since then she has been working full-time at the Wesleyan Nursing Home in Georgetown, Texas.)*

Robert Hunt Morris II and Jeanne Elizabeth (Sokol) Morris, with children *(left to right):* Virginia Rose, Joseph Edward, and Carl David. Photo taken 1991.

Jeanne and Robert live in Leander, Texas, and have three children: Joseph "Joe" (b. 1973), Virginia "Ginnie" (b. 1977), and Carl David (b. 1980). All are in public school. Joe, due to graduate from high school in 1991, has been excelling academically and winning awards in music (bassoon and trombone). (*UPDATE 1991: Joe graduated from Leander High School in May, 1991, as valedictorian and recipient of the overall Science Award. He has accepted a scholarship/work-study package to Baylor University in Waco, Texas, beginning in fall 1991. He will work toward a Bachelor of Music degree and feels called to the Christian ministry. In summer 1991 he is working fulltime at G&S Typesetters, principally in the camera department.*)

Lillie Katherine

Lillie graduated from Medina High in 1962 and from UT-Martin in 1966 with a B.A. in elementary education. She began teaching in DeKalb County, Georgia, where she met Charles Cate from Springville, Tennessee (near Paris). Charles holds a B.S. degree in art education from Murray State University (Kentucky). Both were employed as teachers when they met as well as when they married in 1969. After their first child, Tom, was born in 1971, they moved to Paris, Tennessee, where they still live today. Christy, their second child, was born in 1973.

Charles taught art and photography at Henry County High School for eight years. He obtained his masters in 1972 and completed his "45 above" in 1983. Today he is principal of the Springville Elementary School, part-time photographer, and also a preacher and teacher in the Church of Christ.

Lillie, after Tom was born, stayed home until both her children were in school. Then she began substitute teaching, and in 1988 obtained her certification in library science from UT-Martin. She is now (spring 1990) completing her first year as librarian for grades K-1 in a Paris elementary school.

Tom Cate (spring 1990) is completing his first year at Harding University in Searcy, Arkansas; Christy is completing her junior year at Henry County High School. (*UPDATE 1991: Christy, graduated valedictorian of her class at Henry County High School in Paris, Tennessee. She has a scholarship to Harding University, where Tom continues his studies.*)

Lillie Katherine and Charles Cate, with children Tom and Christy. Photo taken 1991.

CHAPTER XXI

MY SISTER AND BROTHERS[1]

I was the first of four children born to Joseph and Bernice Morris, and have one sister and two brothers, all living at the present time (1990).

Evelyn Clair (Morris) Key

Evelyn finished high school and completed two years of college before marrying Sy Mincey of Jackson, Tennessee. She gave birth to one son, Bobby Joe. Sy was a plasterer, applying stucco exteriors to houses. Later he became a founder of Royal Casket Company in Jackson. Sy died of a stroke in 1962, at 59 years of age. Evelyn remarried, but eventually her second husband, Ike Key, died also. Today she lives at St. Mary's Manor in Jackson.

Bobby Joe Mincey was an outstanding football and baseball player in high school. He considered a professional sports career, but joined the Air Force instead. While stationed in Japan, he met Jean Alexander, and they married in 1960. They helped each other through college and eventually had three children: a daughter, Evelyn, and two sons, John and Brian.

Bobby Joe settled his family in Springfield, Missouri. He worked as a high school coach and guidance counselor, while also pastoring a Baptist church. At 51 years of age, and with no prior history of serious illness, he died of a heart attack. His widow, Jean, is now in DeKalb, Illinois, completing her doctoral degree in business education: Their daughter Evelyn married Ricky Gonser and lives in Redwood, California; John is in the Air Force; and Brian is working.

(UPDATE 1991: In June 1990, Bobby Joe's widow, Jean, married Roger Mausehund. They now live in Hanover Park, Illinois. Both teach;

Roger is head of the business department at Leyden High School near O'Hare Airport, and Jean teaches business communication at Northern Illinois University. Daughter Evelyn and her husband Ricky now have three children (Jeannie, seven; Naomi, five; and Charles Joseph, born January 1991). Jean's son John served in Operation Desert Storm; he is loadmaster on a C-5 transport plane, based at Dover AFB in Delaware. Brian is a store manager in Springfield, Missouri, and Jean writes that he "looks more and more like Bobby every year.")

John Edward Morris

John is the brother nearest to my age. He graduated from Gibson High School in 1930, then attended Western Kentucky State Teachers' College in Bowling Green, Kentucky, while living with our aunt, Mayme Morris Buckberry. After obtaining his B.A. degree in 1934, he returned to Gibson, obtained his teaching certificate through summer studies at Union University, and taught two years in the Gibson school. In the fall of 1936, he again went to Kentucky, where he attended the Bowling Green Business University, and in 1938 was awarded the B.S. degree in Commerce with a major in higher accounting. Returning once again to Gibson, he kept books for Partee & Bass Fruit Company for several months. In 1939, he accepted a position with the Gibson County Electric Membership Corporation, which supplies electricity to northwestern Tennessee, and that same year married Muzzette Booker of Gibson.

When the U.S. entered World War II, John was drafted into the Army and assigned to the Quartermaster Corps. He served in Africa, Italy, France, and Germany. After V-E Day, he was transferred to Berlin (there obtaining souvenirs from Hitler's headquarters) and served there until December 1945.

In January 1946 John was discharged after close to three years of military service. Returning to work with the Electric Corporation, he continued in their service until retirement in 1977. During his 35 years with them, he served as accountant in the Trenton office until 1949; as district manager in the Alamo, Tennessee, office until 1952; and as district manager in the Union City, Tennessee, office until 1977.

Following his official retirement, John has kept busy. For 15 years he has delivered flowers part-time with a local flower shop, and from 1983 to 1990 he worked three days a week with Sage Furniture and Appliances. Besides his employment, John has been an active member in the Baptist church, serving as deacon and Sunday School worker since 1938.

John and Muzzette have two children, Kenneth (b. 1947) and Jozette (b. 1953). Ken has remained single, living with his parents in Union City, and has worked some 20 years for Goodyear Tires. Jozette married Jim Sitko, and they live in Houston, Texas. She is a nurse in a small clinic, and he is manager and part owner of 4J's, Inc., an engineering firm that also produces steel pre-fabs for construction.

In 1989, John and Muzzette celebrated their 50th wedding anniversary.

Robert Morris with his siblings Evelyn, John, and Guy, in 1980. Photo by LLM.

Guy Franklin Morris

Like John, Guy went to Bowling Green, Kentucky, after high school, and he, too, obtained a degree at Bowling Green Business College. Guy returned to Gibson and married Sue Morgan of McKenzie, Tennessee, in 1938. For many years, Guy and Sue lived in the house that Papa and Mama had occupied and where I had been born.

Guy maintained the family farm for a number of years, also working for James Atkins in appliances, handling farm produce, and for the cotton gin, all in Gibson. After my friend Arthur Parrish was elected Gibson County trustee, I suggested that he consider Guy for his assistant. Arthur did appoint Guy to this position, and they worked together during Arthur's two four-year terms. Guy then ran for the trustee office, was elected, and eventually accumulated 21 years of service in the courthouse in Trenton, including his period as assistant trustee.

Sue taught third grade in Gibson until she retired. She and Guy cared for Papa during the last years of his life, moving into Dr. Hunt's former home to do so. They have done extensive remodeling in the old home place, which was built in 1889, and they remain there today.

Their one son, Frank, obtained his bachelor's degree from Memphis State University, then joined the Army, where he had six months' basic training in Fort Jackson, South Carolina. Following this, he served in the Air Force National Guard for six years. In 1963, he began working for International Harvester and that same year married Barbara Buckingham from Brazil, Tennessee. Frank has stayed with his original employer ever since, but in 1985 Tenneco Corporation bought International Harvester and renamed it Case International. Frank has had to relocate several times with his work: West Memphis, Arkansas; Greenwood, Mississippi; Lawrenceburg, Tennessee; Blytheville, Arkansas; Memphis (Germantown), Tennessee; Dallas; and finally Tyler, Texas. Soon he is to move again, this time to Edmond, Oklahoma.

Frank and Barbara have one daughter, Karen, who went to the University of Texas in Austin for one year, and this past year has lived at home in Tyler while attending a local college.

(UPDATE 1991: Karen is currently attending the University of North Texas in Denton, Texas [near where her great-great-Aunt Mildred lived until her death in April 1991]. She is majoring in community services.)

Robert Morris II joins his cousin Frank Morris to celebrate "Ant" Mildred's ninetieth birthday on May 6, 1989. (See chapter 1, footnote no. 8, on Aunt Mildred.) *Seated, left to right:* Jeanne, Barbara, and Mildred Morris. *Standing behind them:* Robert, Frank, Virginia, Joe, and Carl Morris.

CHAPTER XXII

FRIENDS PAST AND PRESENT

SOME WHO ARE NOW GONE

EDITOR'S NOTE: By asking Dad about his best friends, I wanted to acknowledge the importance of friendships in his life and to recognize those individuals and families he felt especially close to. Unfortunately, he recorded these memories while riding in the car with Mother, Una, and myself. This was on the way to the airport in Nashville in September 1989, following his 85th birthday celebration. He had limited time to reflect, and some of the names were suggested to him rather than coming forth spontaneously. It follows that the information obtained is certainly partial, and possibly skewed. Omitted are persons who obviously should have been included, and we genuinely regret this. I further regret that, while most of the chapters in this book were reviewed by Dad before he died, this one, coming last, did not receive the benefit of his closer inspection.

In fact, several members of the immediate family did make an effort to list the names of "close and faithful friends" of Dr. Morris, but the results were less than satisfactory: The list kept growing and growing, as we tried to make it sufficiently inclusive, until it became almost meaningless. Even then it omitted, for example, most members of his Sunday School class. Where would we stop? At best, a list we would construct would reflect our own perceptions, not Dad's, and no doubt many who consider themselves his friends would still be left out.

Having said all this, I trust that what follows, in Dad's own words, (except for a few silent corrections of fact), is of some value. Several notes have been added by family and are printed in italics to identify them.

My closest friends have always been my relatives, so after my wife and my deceased parents and grandparents, I consider my sister Evelyn, my brothers John and Guy, and my Aunt Mildred in Texas, to be my closest friends. But I have been blessed with many other friends, and first I will tell of some no longer with us:

Travis James

He taught my Sunday School class for years when I was a boy. He would invite our class to his home for Christmas entertainment: food, and games of dominoes and Rook. In the summer, he would carry us to the bottomland out from Brownsville, Tennessee, to camp out for two or three days. He fixed up the bed of his old truck with benches, and we'd have a glorious time.

Right after Lillie and I were married, I had Travis make some of my kitchen furniture: a breadboard, a roiling pin, two tables, and an open bookcase. He used the finest poplar lumber to build those tables; Una Deane was born on the larger and Brenda on the smaller of these.

All my life, until he died, I considered Travis James a close friend, someone I could go to for counsel.

Dr. Rozzell

He was the one doctor remaining in Gibson after Dr. Hunt stopped practicing medicine. He was a good Christian man—kind and considerate; willing to help anyone, poor or rich. I enjoyed talking and being associated with him.

Dr. Steven Byars

I first met Dr. Byars while we were both in medical school and our future wives were both in nurse's training. Following Dr. Waller's death in Spring Creek, I insisted on Dr. Byars coming here; I could not keep up with the demands on me to go to Oakfield, Lavinia, Spring Creek and Milan.

Steven stayed in Spring Creek several years, then went to Corinth, Mississippi. During World War II he moved to Jasper, Tennessee, so that his wife and children could be near relatives while he served overseas. He joined the U.S. Army and served in Italy. After the war, Dr. Byars joined the Public Health Service, remaining with them for the rest of his career. He spent a number of years in Union City, Tennessee, then in Monroe, Georgia. Finally he was transferred to LaGrange, Georgia, where he remained until his death just a few years back.

I delivered Joe, one of the Byars' children, in Spring Creek, and Dr. Byars attended the birth of my daughter Brenda. Lillie May and I have visited the Byars at least once in every place they have had a home, and Steven and his wife Edna Earl once treated us to a long and enjoyable trip out West, which I have mentioned in the chapter on "Travel, and World War II." In 1986 we attended their Golden Wedding Anniversary celebration. Our last visit in their home shortly preceded Dr. Byars' death. We still correspond with Edna Earl, who lives with her son Joe in LaGrange today.

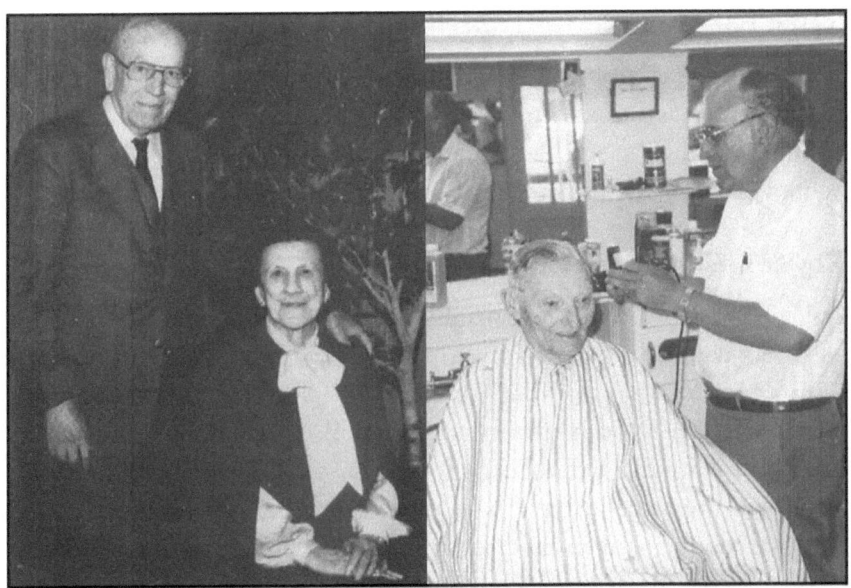

Especially dear friends of Dr. Morris. *Left:* Steven and Edna Earl Byars, who respectively attended medical school and nursing school with Dr. and Mrs. Morris, and became lifelong friends. They celebrated their golden wedding anniversary in 1986, with the Morrises attending. *Right:* Bobby Don Harris, in his barber shop across the street from Jackson General Hospital, cutting Dr. Morris's hair. Here in 1988. Photo by LLM. (Bobby Don now teaches the Sunday School class that Dr. Morris taught for 50 years.)

Dr. Weldon Oliver

Dr. Oliver was the only practicing physician in Medina when I came here in 1937. We became close friends, and I have written about him at some length in the chapter on "Decision to Move." Even in his practice he was unselfish and non-competitive; I never felt he was jealous of my growing practice.

Henry Hester

Henry was our former pharmacist in Medina and a close friend, now deceased. I've mentioned him elsewhere.

FRIENDS IN MEDINA

Space would fail me to tell of all the people we know and love in Medina, but I will mention some of my closest friends here:

Ralph Barnwell

Ralph is a friend I trust and depend on. I feel toward Ralph nearly as I would toward my brother. I delivered his children: a daughter, then a son, and finally twins. Ralph was in my Sunday School class for many years until I recently stepped down as teacher.

Roy & Georgia Mae Graves

We are close neighbors, with only two houses between us, and we enjoy a close friendship. I'd always talk to Roy whenever I went down to buy gas at his garage, and he serviced my cars until his retirement. We're both members of First Baptist Church, and he has been in my Sunday School class for many years. Raising children who were near the same age and who played together help draw us closer. Roy has done many minor services in my house, such as electrical repairs. Recently he has had to stop because of illness. His son Reed has continued to help me as Roy used to.

(UPDATE 1991: Roy died in November 1990. Dr. Morris viewed Roy's body at the funeral home, and Reed's wife Joyce says she heard him exclaim, "Roy went on just a few days before I did!" This occurred before Dr. Morris was diagnosed with cancer, and approximately six weeks before his death.)

Arthur Parrish

My relationship with Arthur is very different from that with Roy, but we have been equally close. I spoke to Arthur on my brother Guy's behalf when Arthur was county trustee, and he took Guy on as his deputy. To this day, Arthur often stops by my house. I've watched both of his open heart operations—one in Memphis, and the other one, 11 or 12 years later, in Jackson. I have tended him in many other sicknesses, and have tended his wife, Mutt. I delivered their son John, as well as Mutt's two older boys, Bill and Jere.

Paul Gowan

Paul is my next-door neighbor. We have been acquaintances and friends since I first moved to Medina, when his house was across the street from ours and he was a close friend of Dr.

Oliver's son Wilbur. (In fact, I had met Paul several years before that, when I used to come courting in Medina.)

Paul married Nancy Wright. After our move to Main Street, Paul and Nancy lived in the second house south of us. Many years later, after Nancy's aunt died, they moved into her house next door. Nancy was very sweet to us; I don't know how many times she has cut my hair and washed my head. She died in 1989, and Paul still mourns for her; fortunately his older daughter Jerrie and one granddaughter live right beside his house.

Abe & Beulah Utley

For nearly 50 years, Abe and Beulah were our next-door neighbors on the north, and we have also been good friends. We watched their two sons, Robert Vernon and Lloyd Allen, grow up. Abe was working then for the state tax department. After retiring from state service, Abe stayed home day and night; like me, he would mainly work his garden, and we always had a friendly rivalry to see who could grow the better garden. (Both of us farmed in our early years.)

Tragedy entered Abe's life when Robert Vernon was found dead in his home in Jackson, Tennessee. Another tragedy occurred when Lloyd Allen's wife had a very rare head condition several years ago from which she died, leaving four children. Now Abe and Beulah both are in a nursing home in Milan; Paul and I visit them, and their condition saddens us.

(UPDATE 1991: Beulah died on January 31, 1991, about five weeks after Dr. Morris.)

Bobby Don Harris

Bobby Don is the same age as our oldest daughter Una. He is such a close friend that I let him cut the hair off my head! He is kind to me, carrying me places with him, inviting me to go with them. His wife Patricia has been good to us, bringing us peas and corn and sweet potatoes.

Reau & Rebecca Graves

We have had close relations with Reau and Rebecca from the time Reau was working in the garage with his brother Roy. I delivered their two children, and their son Reau Junior's first child also.

Finis & Marie Sims

The Sims lived two doors north of us for many years, then built on a lot in front of the Methodist Church. Finis has always come to me about their health needs, and still does today.

Ed & Thelma Tatum

We have developed a close friendship, and I was with Ed when he had open-heart surgery.

Elton & Jamie McDonald

Our friendship has grown through the years, and I have delivered their children and cared for their family medically. Elton will knock on our door, then walk right on in the house, like family. Although we've argued religion a lot (I Baptist, he Church of Christ), we have a real friendship. Once he even carried Lillie May and me down to Florence, Alabama.

Mrs. Jackie Rowlett

She was a close friend, and lived next door to our first home in Medina. Her children, Brooks and Latisha, are still close to us.

Cora Sims

I've known Cora and her children ever since I've been in Medina, and have been in her home many a time.

(UPDATE 1991: Cora died on December 30, 1990, the same day that Dr. Morris was buried.)

MEDICAL FRIENDS

Dr. Tom West

Dr. West, now deceased, was one of my closest friends. He resided in Memphis, where he was resident surgeon at Memphis General Hospital while I was interning, and later did a residency in the Leihey Clinic. He came back to Memphis and associated with Dr. Lucius McGee, head of surgery at UT Medical School. When Dr. McGee died, Tom took over his office and continued his practice until Tom himself died.

In all my years of practice, when I had any patient needing unusual or life-threatening surgery, I would call Tom West and say "Tom, I've got someone for you. I think he has got so-and-so." And he would say, "Send him on down," never asking if they were able to pay. When Lillie and I attended Mid-South medical meetings in Memphis, we would visit in his home and eat breakfast with his children.

(LLM: While in the hospital with fever and pneumonia, Dr. Morris once called for Dr. West.)

Dr. Glen Batten & Dr. John Pierce

I became closely associated with both these men in my practice. Dr. Batten was in the old Memorial Hospital. Whenever I had a surgical case, I'd call him, and he'd say, "Send him in." Whenever I had a medical case, I'd call John Pierce, who was Dr. Batten's associate. John and I were good friends; he even delivered our daughter Lillie Katherine in Doctor's Hospital.

Often when I would have to go to Jackson of a morning, I would stop at Dr. Pierce's home and eat breakfast with him and his family. His wife was pleasant and made visits enjoyable.

Dr. Hughes Chandler

I knew Hughes during his medical schooling and residency in Memphis. I sent him a lot of cases to Jackson General, and many times assisted him in surgery.

Dr. G. Baker Hubbard

Dr. Hubbard has been a close friend. For many years he was the only orthopedic surgeon in Jackson, dealing with fractured hips and other bones. The patients I sent to him all did well. He did not retire until January 1, 1990, when he was well over 70 years old. He used to be at Jackson Clinic each morning except Thursday. Especially if I had any minor surgery patients, I would just give them a note saying to see Dr. Baker Hubbard, and he would receive them.

Dr. Riddler

Dr. Riddler is another close friend, and I have worked with him on a lot of surgical cases. At one time I had him take a skin cancer off the back of my hand. He did a lot of cosmetic surgery; he was also good at mesenteric thrombosis and gall bladder operations, and any other surgery.

Dr. George Dodson

Dr. Dodson has been a close associate. I thought he was a sound, common-sense surgeon, with good skill. Early in my practice I told him, "George, I'm sending a case over here, Phillip Replogle. And if you'll just treat him and he does well, you'll have a third or more of the practice in Medina, because there are a lot of Replogles and their relatives in the community." His treatment of Phillip Replogle was successful, and I never had trouble getting a patient to go see him.

It is sad to see George today, a patient in the Alzheimer unit behind the Jackson Clinic. One day, when he was in the hospital being treated for pneumonia, I visited his room, and he exclaimed, "Bob!" But he has never carried on any further conversation with me then or since. A nurse is constantly by his side.

(Some physician friends omitted above, as recalled by family members: H. P. Clemmer, James Fields, Leland Johnston, P. D. Jones, Henry Moore, Lamb Myhr, Charles Stauffer, George Thomas, and Paul Wylie. We also want to mention the family dentist of many years, Robert P. Denney.)

FRIENDS FROM CHILDHOOD

J. C. & Letona Warmath

We were all close friends from childhood; Letona's maiden name was Lessenberry. I delivered their two children while I was in Gibson. To this day, I think a lot of them. Letona has moved to San Antonio, Texas, since her husband's death.

Irene Thomas

Irene has always been a close friend. Her father and mine were raised in the same church and community; they attended the same school, Oakview, and lived across the street from one another all their lives. I've been in the home of Robert Guy and Irene many a time. To this day I send her a Christmas card.

Last prescription written by Dr. Morris, a little more than two weeks before his death.

Last prescription written by Dr. Morris, a little more than two weeks before his death.

AFTERWORD
Into Eternity

Dr. Robert Hunt Morris died on December 27, 1990, following six weeks of treatment for pancreatic lymphoma, at the age of 86 years, three months, and one day. He was buried on December 30, 1990, in the Hunt-Morris family plot in White Rose Cemetery, Gibson, Tennessee; the following day would have been his and Lillie May's 55th wedding anniversary.

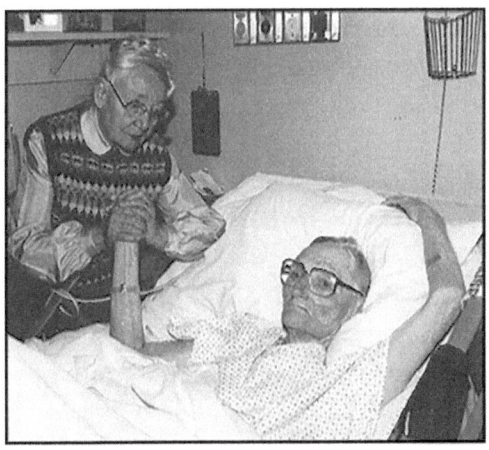

Dr. Morris during his final illness, tended by his faithful mate of nearly 55 years, Lillie May. Here in Nov. 1990, photo by RMII.

FROM OBITUARY IN THE *MEDINA STAR*[1]

Funeral services for Dr. Robert Hunt Morris, age 86, were held at 2:00 p.m. Sunday, December 30, at the Medina First Baptist Church, with Rev. Ronnie Gay and Rev. John Pippin officiating. Burial followed in White Rose Cemetery near Gibson, with Replogle-Lawrence Funeral Home in charge of arrangements....

Serving as pallbearers were grandsons William Craig Grant [*in absentia*], Melton Crosby Ambrose, Bryant Edwin Nulter, James Andrew Grant, Michael Clarence Ambrose, Richie Alan Ambrose, Robert Browning Grant, Charles Thomas Cate II, Joseph Edward Morris, John Robert Ambrose, and Carl David Morris.

Serving as honorary pallbearers were Medina First Baptist deacons, Seekers Sunday School Class members, and members of the Medical Association.

HIS FINAL HOURS[2]

2:30 a.m., Wednesday, December 26, 1990—I was home alone, asleep since 6 p.m., after riding on home from the hospital with Lil's family (she was home sick Christmas day). Trebor was with her daddy. She called to let me know that he was calling, "Lillie, Mama". Elton and Denny McDonald had me there in minutes. Robert was relaxing. I kissed his forehead. Trebor took her bedding to the day room. Again, we were together alone and rested until 8 a.m. Dr. Lewis came announcing his decision for no more chemotherapy without a subclavian cut down for feedings. Dr. Morris' Living Will ruled that out. Weakness overwhelmed his frail 114 lb. body. There was no strength to lift his eyelids or speak above a whisper. Mid-afternoon Una Deane found his I.V. out; his veins were collapsed.[3] Intravenous was discontinued. Bessie Childress, her brother, Odell Smith, and his wife, Marilyn, came to visit (en route home from having Christmas with their family in Corinth, MS). Our last invitation out to a good home cooked meal was with them, in early fall.

Una came back from mailing a letter to her son William (in the Navy). During this time Bobby Don Harris came. Shortly afterward, Dr. Morris spoke in an inaudible voice we struggled to understand. I asked, "Do you want Bobby to shave you?" With all the life in him, he whispered, "Yes." That Bobby did, combed his hair, and straightened his part. (Loose hair came out with every stroke of the comb.). A surge of strength made audible his "Thank you, Bobby." Several times that fall Bobby had cut his hair at home gratis. Again, thank you.

Lonnie Kee was there when Dr. Myhr came. He said, "I'll see you in the morning." A constant quiver of the chin had set in. He called,

"Mama". I clasped his right hand into both of mine. His lips quivered as he said, "I love you. I appreciate you."

Nurses came in to change linens and turn him. I rubbed his back with Swiss Formula lotion and sprinkled his draw sheet with Calsadene powder. I requested his "I.M." injection of Haldol be given for relaxation. It was given.

With his hands clasped, he prayed, "Father, let me go." My hand cupped his forehead. He whispered, "Mama, go with me." A death tear trickled from his right eye. As I was blotting it with a Puff, the phone rang. Brenda called from Huntsville to let her Daddy know that she, Ed, Kelley, and Elvis were in special prayer for him. As I hung up the receiver, Robert whispered, "Mama, help me pray my prayers. Help me pray, Mama." I did. Following a period of quiet time, he again called, "MAMA". The tone of his voice caused me to ask, "Do you mean me or Mama Bee?" His reply was, "My mama. Mama, Mama, I'm coming."

At midnight he was turned again to his right side. His temperature, blood pressure, and pulse were normal. His breathing was rapid and labored. At 3 a.m. his breathing was less labored and slower. His arms were cold to his elbows.

At 7:05 a.m., Thursday, December 27, 1990, I read aloud the Forty-third Psalm. His spirit left his body, leaving behind a host of family and friends who loved him. He loved and served us all; our lives are richer for having him. His family could not have received more loving support anywhere on earth at any period of history. I stand amazed at God's timing of it all.

"Victory in Jesus" was the theme of the message he left us all. I'm so grateful to God for having made him OURS.

Sincerely, Lillie

SHARED THOUGHTS FROM THE JOURNAL OF GRANDDAUGHTER CHRISTY MARIE CATE[4]

September 26, 1989

He turned 85 today. His motions still carry in that rhythmic pattern that was set so long ago. Yes, the pace has slowed some over the years, but the sparkle in the eye mirrors the youth that's still remembered. Timeless moments are captivated in that sparkle, and oh what stories they could tell!

He sits silently, soaking in what the last eight-and-a-half decades have dealt him. The faint hint of a curve around his lips says there were the good and the bad, but life has been fair and satisfactory. He can't help but delighting in the meaning of those days when he ran through the yard like his four-year-old great-grandson does.

A slight blush of color enters his hollowed cheeks as he fondly recalls that cherished moment of his first date in the family "horse and buggy". In the realities of his mind, it was only yesterday that he awkwardly leaned over and gave Lillie May a peck on the cheek. The old man relishes in the thoughts of days when age meant nothing.

The softly sung lines of "Happy Birthday" begin to intensify as they slowly drag him back from his reverie. His back seems to curl slightly at the disappointment at being disturbed from his stroll down memory lane. Though the physical body has weakened, the soul and character within still burst with fiery passion to continue, and so they shall. As long as it is God's will, he will continue to fuel them with memories, but even when he's gone, a tiny part of his inner self will survive and be carried on through the will of those he has known and loved. Each one has been touched in some way by him that they will remember and cherish as part of themselves, then in turn, relinquish it to another who will continue the chain of his never-dying spirit.

December 27, 1990 [Written at] 12:48 a.m. on December 28, 1990

He died today. Three months into his 87th year, he left this old world for a better one. His physical body was tired and weary after traveling eight-and- a-half decades amongst an imperfect race of humanity. All strength had seeped away, and the cruel thief called cancer had aided in destroying the vitality of the dear old "codger".

No longer does he exist in whole, but his mannerisms, characteristics, personality traits, and memories will forever exist in parts. Most prominently can they be found in his five children—four girls and a boy. Seventeen grandchildren and seven great-grandchildren will continue to spread his thoughts and keep his spirit alive. "Oh shucks, Lillie May, we don't need to do that!" "Be sure those children turn those lights off in that attic, do you hear me now?" "Ha, ha, well I'll be cat nipples! "Honey give me just a little cream with some chocolate." "Oh, I don't know, maybe just a little Coca- Cola will be all right!" "Gracious Father we want to thank thee for this day . . . and bless my Una, my Trebor, my Brenda, my Lillie, and my Robert." "Honey give me just a little sugar . . . hmmm, thank you honey, that cheek is so sweet." "Just be sure you're saved, honey, be sure you're saved!" And finally, "I . . . . . . (l)ove . . . . . . (y)ou!" (The most beautiful words of all!)

I don't ever want to forget, Papaw. I loved you, I still love you, and I'll always love you!!! Yes, Papaw, there *is* "Victory in Jesus"!

EXCERPT FROM ROBERT II'S FAMILY LETTER OF JANUARY, 1991

A sizable number of the community came to view Dad's body, and in spite of the heavily overcast day and the intermittent rain, the Baptist church was nearly full at his memorial service. In fact, the gloom and rain seemed appropriate, since his death was a loss not only to his large family (5 children, 17 grandchildren, 7 great-grandchildren, as well as two brothers and one sister still living), but in a real way was also a loss to the church, where for a half-century he had served as deacon and as teacher of a men's Bible class, and to the community that he had served faithfully for over 50 years as its only doctor (he wrote his last prescription only weeks before his death).

Cancer destroyed Dad's body, but this is our hope: "We believe that Jesus died and rose again and so we believe that God will bring with Jesus those who have fallen asleep in him" (I Thess. 4:15). On Sunday morning before the funeral, some 20 of us gathered in the family home in Medina and had a participatory worship service. We read scripture, shared memories and perspectives on Dad, and sang. Finally, we took communion together, then stood and sang 'Victory in Jesus' (one of Dad's favorites, and a family theme song). The chorus reads:

O victory in Jesus, my Savior, forever,
He sought me and bought me with his redeeming blood;
He loved me ere I knew him, and all my love is due him,
He plunged me to victory beneath the cleansing flood.

STATEMENT READ AT GRAVESIDE SERVICE[5]

We believe in one God the Father All-sovereign, maker of heaven and earth, and of all things visible and invisible;

And in one Lord Jesus Christ, the only begotten Son of God, Begotten of the Father before all the ages, Light of Light, true God of true God, begotten not made, of one substance with the Father, through whom all things were made; who for us men and for our salvation came down from the heavens, and was made flesh of the Holy Spirit and the Virgin Mary, and became man, and was crucified for us under Pontius Pilate, and suffered and was buried, and rose again on the third day according to the Scriptures, and ascended into the heavens, and sitteth on the right hand of the Father, and cometh again with glory to judge living and dead, of whose kingdom there shall be no end;

And in the Holy Spirit, the Lord and the Life-giver, that proceedeth from the Father, who with Father and Son is worshipped together and glorified together, who spake through the prophets;

In one holy Catholic [universal, orthodox] and Apostolic Church;

We acknowledge one baptism unto remission of sins. We look for a resurrection of the dead, and the life of the age to come.

Victory In Jesus

E. M. B.   E. M. Bartlett

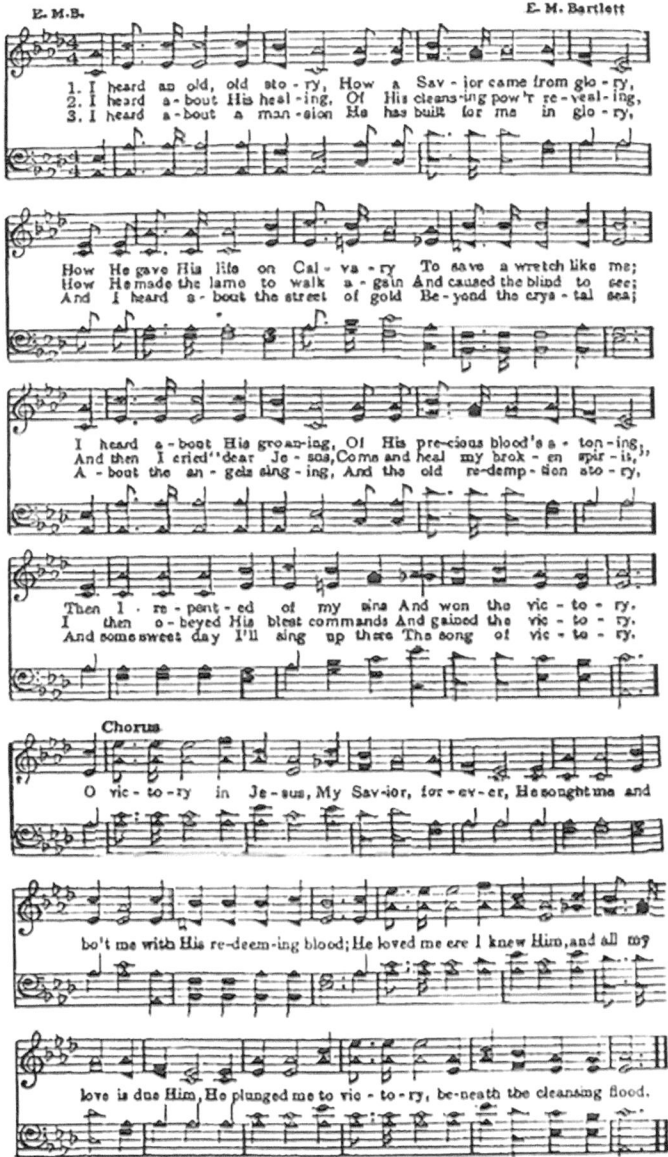

ADDENDUM
by Brenda Morris Nulter

When my husband Ed and I were first dating, Dad said, "If you make your bed, you must lie in it!" When Ed came to the table to eat, Dad would say, "Don't feed him too much; he might come back!" But Dad learned to love Ed and his family. Although they were poor, they were honest, hard- working, inventive, and could do many kinds of work: carpentry, electrical, automotive, etc. Ed, himself a champion golfer in high school and later a basketball coach, loved to watch sports with Dad, and he always sought financial advice from him. When we were buying our house, we drew upon our mutual funds for down payment and borrowed the cash value of my whole-life insurance, provided by Dad, for the rest. We registered the loan in the courthouse at 8% interest.

In nine years we paid it off, and thus were able to send our three children to college. I recall how Dad helped me with the diagnosis of our son Bryant's condition when he was born with congenital aganglionic megacolon or Hirschsprung's disease. I went back to the hospital where I had received my med tech degree and had given birth to my first two children. I would find Bryant's bedding wet after I nursed and burped him, and I showed Dad his yellow, birdseed-like BMs. Dad examined him and said, "Look at the expression on his face!" After palpating three times across his abdomen he said, "Here is where his obstruction is." Months later, after taking Bryant to the Children's Hospital in Birmingham for X- rays, then colostomy surgery in his lower left abdomen, the surgery had to be repeated much higher up, exactly where Dad had said the obstruction was.

One evening a Mr. Parrish came to our family home complaining of shoulder pain. After examining him, Dad said, "I think you're having a heart attack." Dad sent him to Jackson to a specialist. Mr. Parrish came back and said, "They don't see any evidence for a heart problem." Dad said, "From my experience, that is what I think." Mr. Parrish returned once or twice for Dad to send him back to the specialist. When he appeared again for an exam, Dad gave him medicine for angina. Soon Mr. Parrish died of a heart attack.

I recall when "brother-in-love" Charlie kept having some unusual symptoms. He would sweat for no apparent reason and would go to sleep anytime he lay down. His eyes were bloodshot and he always ran a low- grade fever. A doctor in Paris, Tennessee, diagnosed it as pleurisy. Dad took him to Jackson, and he was diagnosed there as having shingles. On the way out Dad said, "I don't know what you have, but I know it's not that." Dad sent him to a Memphis doctor, who put him in the hospital. Dad went down to visit and looked at Charlie's chart. It said everything looked good. Dad threw the chart down and said, "I ordered a lead-poisoning test!" The nurse scurried to get it ordered, and the test came back positive. Charlie had gotten lead poisoning from the oil paints and pottery he worked with in his art classes.

One day when I was about 10, Dad took me to the hospital where he had sent twins that were premature and each weighed less than two pounds. They had gauze on their eyes and looked so tiny to me. They were under the care of a pediatrician, but Dad wanted to check on their welfare. The girls survived, but were blind from the high oxygen content in the incubator.

One day Dad told us about an unusual delivery he had done that day. He said it was a "superimposed pregnancy." The lady had conceived a second child while pregnant. The babies were conceived a month or two apart. He said most OB/GYN physicians would never see this in their lifetime.

Dad's last call: Dad had quit regular practice 20 years before and was dying of pancreatic lymphoma. Mr. Foutch's wife called for the third time to ask Dad to come out to Christmasville Road. Dad kept saying, "I just can't go!" I said, "Dad, I'll drive you and carry your bag." He said, "I don't think I can get up to the house." I took him, and he found Mr. Foutch in bed with a stroke. He gave him medicine and called in a doctor to see him either that evening or the next morning, since the

98-year-old gentleman was stable and resting. As I drove back home, Dad said, "I'm a much sicker man than he is." I said, "I know, Dad."

He proceeded to tell me about his finances: taxes and investments. He didn't think Mom could handle it all. I told him I did my own and would be able to handle them. He asked me to take care of sister Una until she reached 60 years of age and could draw a widow's Social Security pension. A robust 1990s market allowed Mom to do this. Praise be to God!

ENDNOTES

Foreword by Robert Morris II, and Letters from Each of His Children

[1] *Jackson* Sun (Jackson, Tenn.), December 30, 1990. Used by permission.

Family Background

[1] According to tombstones in White Rose Cemetery, Gibson, Tennessee, the years of birth and death of these individuals are:

Joseph Edward Morris 1881-1967
Bernice Hunt Morris 1875-1939
John Peter Morris 1852-1923
Sarah Chandler Morris 1844-1897
Dr. Robert Hardy Hunt 1845-1936
Lisa Hurt Hunt was buried near the entry gate to Eldad Cemetery (per LLM); dates were not obtained for her.

[2] This paragraph is adapted from an entry originally written by LLM in *Families and History of Gibson County, Tennessee, to 1989*, compiled by Lee-Davis United Daughters of the Confederacy Historical Society, Milan, TN (Salem, WV: Wadsworth Publishing Company, 1990), p. 193. Used by permission of the Lee-Davis U.D.C. Historical Society.

[3] *LLM:* R. H. Hunt attended the University of Nashville Medical School, forerunner of both the Vanderbilt and the University of Tennessee schools of medicine. Gibson County historians give the name of "Dr. L. M. McAlily" as the man with whom young doctors trained during this period of Gibson County history. The sheepskin diploma Dr. Hunt received remained in a tin cylinder during his lifetime; LLM later had it framed, and it still hangs over her television as it did during Dr. Morris's lifetime. It measures 25½ × 21½ inches.

[4] Information in this last sentence was supplied by Dr. Morris's brother, John Morris.

[5] *LLM:* According to Will Freeman (personal conversation), his stepfather John Peter Morris told him the Morrises were of English ancestry, that they came to

Tennessee from North Carolina, and that he himself was directly descended from a man who married a Cherokee woman.

6   *LLM:* The Eldad Baptist Church building and records were burned during the Civil War by Yankee soldiers.

7   On Kate and Jack, Mildred Morris (Dr. Robert Morris's half-aunt (see note no. 8 below), interviewed by RMII on her ninetieth birthday (May 6, 1989), said this: "My father drove a surrey, and we went [on Sundays] in the daytime to church in a surrey driven by these two mules. And they were so that they would only go to the church; if you wanted to go some other way, they would have to be led or directed in some way; they would balk at the matter."

8   Dates 1866-1946 for Sally Freeman are on her tombstone in White Rose Cemetery, Gibson, Tennessee. Mildred Morris's age is given here as of summer 1990; she died in April, 1991, less than four months after Dr. Morris, her half-nephew. She would have been 92 on May 6. "Ant" Mildred, as she regularly signed her letters, had a wonderful sense of humor.

9   W. T. today lives in La Mesa, California. Mildred Morris, his half-aunt, remained a close friend of W. T.'s family, and they visited each other until her death. W T.'s son, W. T. Freeman, Jr., attended the memorial service held in Denton for Mildred, where Frank (Guy Morris's son) and RMII met him for the first time. After a career in banking, W. T., Jr. is now studying at Southwest Theological Seminary (Southern Baptist) in Fort Worth. He is married, with a son and a daughter, both in their twenties.

Papa and Mama

1   *RMII:* Joe Morris's character (my generation called him "Pawpaw") impresses me. In fact, he figures in an incident that has had an impact on my life: When, in 1962, I returned from my junior year of college in France, I was a non-believer, seeking for reality. This led to friction with Dad, and an argument erupted between us in front of Morris relatives in Gibson during a holiday visit. Pawpaw gently intervened, telling Dad, "Leave him alone; the Lord will deal with him." Eventually I was drawn back to the Christian faith, but this was after Pawpaw had died. Then I had a vivid dream, in which I saw Pawpaw; we cried and embraced each other. On waking, I knew that I wanted to have the beautiful spirit I had seen in him. This was about the time our first child was conceived, so it was natural to name him after my grandfather.

Verses that Pawpaw quoted to me on several occasions, so I believe they served as a watchword for him, were: "Trust in the Lord with all thine heart, and lean not to thine own understanding; in all thy ways acknowledge Him, and He will direct thy paths" (Proverbs 3:5–6, HCSB).

2   *RMII:* "Much less" here has the opposite of its usual value. I have heard it used this way only a few times in my life. "That-a-way" (stress is on "that") = "that way," as Dad usually pronounced it.

3   Una (Morris) Grant supplies this information: Joseph Edward Morris attended Oakview School in the Gibson community, a private school emphasizing Latin and a classical form of education. He also attended Union University in 1902, rooming with Nestor James. *RMII:* Joe Morris was the valedictorian of his high school class; I remember hearing him recite the opening sentences of his speech.

4   Una (Morris) Grant understands that "Mama Bee" had help with the wash in later years.

My Earliest Memories

1   *LLM:* Until the last few years, Robert said he was six years old when he learned to plow.

Growing Up

1   This paragraph added by RMII, drawing upon various statements made by Dr. Morris.

2   Dad is recalling the style of speech he and other boys in his community would have used in that period.

Sin and Salvation

1   Philippians 3:14 (quoting from memory)

Gibson Baptist Church

1   In her history of Gibson Baptist Church, Sue Morris wrote that after fire destroyed the building on December 6, 1942, the church met in the school cafeteria while the basement of the present building was constructed and covered. The congregation then used the basement until after World War II; the building was dedicated on November 20, 1949.

2   John Morris (Dr. Morris's brother), adds that prayer meetings were also held in this room on Wednesday nights.

3   John Morris says he, too, served for a time as church janitor, for $5 a month; in his opinion (hindsight?) it was not a very good wage.

4   *LLM:* Mary Dawson taught music at Medina High School for several years. The first year that she taught in Medina, there was no music room at the school. We had a piano in our back bedroom, and her pupils came over to our house for their lessons that year.

[5] I Corinthians 2:2 (quoting from memory)

[6] John 14:15, HCSB

[7] I Corinthians 11:25 (quoting from memory)

[8] According to John Morris, the congregation used a common communion cup at that time.

College, and First Attempts at Medical School

[1] Surely he is referring to the teaching of evolution . Strangely, Dad flooded our home with literature such as the *National Geographic* and books on nature that taught evolution. Perhaps he was vicariously seeking further understanding through me, his son, who read these materials. I don't think he read them himself. (RMII)

Internship and Romance

[1] *LLM:* Dr. Morris has combined two separate events here. Dr. Morris and I were already dating when Doris Kirkman visited. "Following Doris's visit, I told Robert to make a choice. If Doris was his choice, we would quit and I would spend my time with someone else. The McElroy episode occurred following my surgery (removal of the coccyx), necessitated by a childhood injury. Robert took off to go home with me for a few days. Doris Kirkman was a home economics major in college and married a Wheeler; she lives in Lexington, Kentucky, has a physician son, and is a Kentucky basketball fan.

[2] Membrane lining the skull, taken from a person who has died.

[3] Born June 6, 1911, in Williston (Fayette County), Tennessee, to Richard Deane Leake (1879– 1948) and Lillie Katherine (Morton) Leake (1884– 1966). Richard Deane Leake was a well contractor. Lillie May later lived in Arlington and in Greenlevel (the old family plantation, north of Collierville). She finished high school at George R. James High School in Shelby County, had one year in home economics at UT-Knoxville, one quarter at Memphis State Teachers' College, and then obtained her associate degree at UT Junior College in Martin, Tennessee. Finally, in 1935, she obtained her B.S. in nursing from the UT School of Nursing in Memphis. Her siblings are: Richard (1913–1990), Tingnal (b. 1916), John (b. 1919), Albert (1925–1977), and Bess (b. 1927). Bess married Vasco Fast.

[4] *LLM:* Farrer Leake's wife, Lena May, is still alive at age 91, and a resident of Wesley Towers in Memphis. His sister Gladys died in late 1989 at the age of 94. Emmajean, sister to Farrer and Gladys, lived to be 97 years old; she made LLM's wedding gown.

[5] Earthquake-resistant structures have since replaced these that were completed in 1936.

Decision to Move

[1] The narrative fails to mention pharmacist Jimmy Williams, who purchased the drugstore in Medina from Henry Hester in April, 1932, and maintained it as a personal business until December 31, 1973. Dr. Williams sold his pharmaceutical business to City Drugs in Humboldt, and his sundries business to Betty Hogue, an employee. The old marble soda fountain, where Dr. Morris got his daily chocolate milkshake "for [his] ulcer," was sold to the Old Country Store in Jackson, Tennessee, and is in use there today. Incidentally, Jimmy Williams' son Larry, who was in the same grade of school as Dr. Morris's daughter Trebor, became a physician. Dr. Larry Williams lives and practices in Trenton, Tennessee, today, where his parents also live in retirement.

[2] Adapted by RMII from article written by Dr. Morris in *Medina Star*, April 18, 1989. Used by permission.

Settling and Practicing in Medina

[1] Dr. Hunt had died in 1936. If there was a cosigner for this loan, it was probably Dr. Morris's father, Joseph, whose wife had inherited Dr. Hunt's property.

[2] LLM denies "selling" Dr. Morris on this idea, as implied here.

[3] Joseph Edward Morris later married Ora Loving (1872–1955; dates from tombstone in White Rose Cemetery, Gibson). *LLM:* Ora was the sister of Mable Faucett, wife of Joe Morris's brother Charlie. Ora's first husband had died; she had an unmarried daughter, Carey Loving. Charlie and Mable had two children; Egbert has died, while Mable is still living in Springfield, Missouri.

[4] *LLM:* Weekly ward rounds, monthly meetings, and special programs earned Dr. Morris many hours of postgraduate credit. He remained a consulting staff member until his death.

[5] *LLM:* From October 1937 until June 1952, the Gibson County Health Department rendered Home Delivery Services. This was a pilot program by the Commonwealth Fund. Dr. Morris delivered several hundred of his babies in the home under this program. Mrs. Irene Markham (first married nurse to be employed by the State of Tennessee) served our part of the county and helped Dr. Morris with many deliveries.

[6] Wingo Campbell recalls being "drafted" several times to drive Dr. Morris on calls out in the country:

> ... I would wait in the car while he made his call inside to the patient.
>
> One night, we were way up in the country near Lavinia. I napped several times and thought he would never come out. Finally, when he did show up,

he said he had a patient in there who gave birth to twins. Believe you me, he was tired and glad he could relax going home with me driving!

(*Medina Star,* Oct. 19, 1990, p. 11; used with permission)

[7] "a-tall" (stress on "tall") = "at all," as Dr. Morris usually pronounced it.

[8] *LLM:* As patients moved away, their confidence was still in their hometown doctor. Calls came from many states, from New York to California, and from as far away as Canada and Mexico, asking for direction and reassurance in their health problems.

Travel, and World War II

[1] Word not understood on tape and never clarified by Dr. Morris. Guesses would be "Ready" or "Aim."

[2] *LLM:* In the 1970s we took several trips with the Senior Citizens and the Harvest Years Center. These included Eureka Springs, Arkansas, and Washington, D.C.

Home Life

[1] Larry Western, a classmate of RMII.

[2] Galatians 5:2 (quoting from memory)

[3] *LLM:* Robert H. was Phi Beta Kappa; Brenda maintained a 4.0 average through high school, college, and graduate school; Una won a Guttenheimer Award; and a UT-Martin professor said Lillie was his "pick of the flock."

[4] *RMII:* I don't remember kneeling, but I do remember, when growing up, a ritual of asking, waiting through his grumbling and questioning, and asking a second or third time, before receiving our modest requests for money. In contrast, as an adult, I found Dad to be very generous, lending me money when I asked for it and giving, without my asking, whenever he sensed a need.

Retirement

[1] *RMII:* I was particularly impressed when, at one point, a speaker asked all those whom Dr. Morris had delivered as babies to rise. It seemed that half of those present stood up.

[2] *LLM:* While Dr. Morris was still in the hospital with prostate surgery, I had the phone taken out of his office. Almost two years later, the building remained as it had been left. I personally sorted books, etc., and, with Larry Darby's help, took a number of books to Jackson State College. Later, the office furniture was brought to our house. The building was rented out as a residence, then sold to Johnny Leake, my nephew, an architect. It now belongs to Boyd King as rental property.

3 "c" is for *cum*, Latin for "with," medical terminology which Dr. Morris used in personal correspondence as well as on prescriptions.

Hobbies and Leisure

1 *LLM:* On January 7, 1991 (a week following Dr. Morris's funeral), Melton and Trebor Ambrose, Una Grant, and I were guests of the Consolidated Medical Association of West Tennessee at a meeting in which Dr. Morris and Dr. George Dodson were memorialized.

2 *LLM:* These meetings rotated between Memphis, Nashville, and Chattanooga. Dr. Morris often attended meetings in Memphis, but never in Chattanooga.

3 Bobby Don Harris was chosen as regular teacher for this class after Dr. Morris became unable to continue teaching in early 1990.

4 *LLM:* Early that day, our next-door neighbor, Abe Utley, drove Dr. Morris to the hospital for an X-ray.

The Coming of Modern Conveniences

1 *RMII:* "Miz Virgie" taught four of us Morris children in the first grade. She still lives in Medina today (1991). Lucy Norvell taught Una Deane in first grade, and Marie Sims taught all of us in the second grade.

2 John Morris remembers their names as Rufus and Mary, not William and Mary.

Observations on Myself

1 Luke 12:15 (quoting from memory)

2 Dr. Morris lived off his income, but saved and invested, especially in dividend life insurances, mutual funds, and stock. These investments became a source of retirement income and of generous gifts to his children and to institutions, as well as providing for Mrs. Morris after his death.

3 Proverbs 3:6, WEB

4 Philippians 4:7 (quoting from memory)

Our Children, Grandchildren, and Great-Grandchildren

1 Supplemented and corrected with information gathered from Dr. Morris's wife and children. Updated through June 1991.

My Sister and Brothers

1 Dr. Morris's memories have been supplemented and corrected with information received from his siblings and from Jean Mausehund.

Afterword: Into Eternity

[1] Article by Marsha Moore Blount, December 31, 1990. Used by permission.

[2] Reprinted by permission from the "Living and Loving with Lillie" column, written by LLM (*Medina Star*, January 31, 1991).

[3] Una Deane recalls the veins being rigid, rather than collapsed.

[4] Reprinted from the special bulletin prepared for Dr. Morris's memorial service, held December 30, 1990, at the First Baptist Church in Medina, Tennessee.

[5] The Nicene Creed, read by Rev. John Pippin.

Dr. Robert H. Morris was born to a simple, pious, hardscrabble farm family in 1904 which owned no tractor or other power machinery. This toughened him for a medical career in a community where he was the only doctor making house calls into the 1970s. People preferred him to the much more expensive hospitals of last resort, not only for money's sake but because of his accurate diagnoses and effective treatment. He delivered, he estimated, 2500 babies in his career, close to 2000 of these in the home, charging a $25 fee. His wife, a registered nurse and an artist, designed a modest, attractive office for him, built in 1950. He kept regular hours there but was subject to interruption day and night, weekends too, whenever there were urgent needs. He had no replacement or backup, and was truly always on call.

Dr. Morris' son, Robert H. Morris II, actually wrote the book, first drafting it from six hours of interviews with his dad, then presenting this draft to him on his 85th birthday. Robert II then recorded two more hours of his dad's memoriies, and they mailed chapters back and forth from Texas to Tennessee for correction and approval until just weeks before Dr. Morris' death. After the doctor died, his wife, daughters, and community members helped complete and correct the details .